DATE DUE

AP 6 '98			
OC 3 '98			
AP 3 '02			
NO 25 03			

DEMCO 38-296

REMARKABLE REMAINS

OF THE ANCIENT PEOPLES OF GUATEMALA

REMARKABLE REMAINS
OF THE
ANCIENT PEOPLES
OF GUATEMALA

By Jacques VanKirk and Parney Bassett-VanKirk

UNIVERSITY OF OKLAHOMA PRESS : NORMAN AND LONDON

VanKirk, Jacques.
  Remarkable remains of the ancient peoples of Guatemala / by Jacques VanKirk
and Parney Bassett-VanKirk.
     p.   cm.
  Includes bibliographical references and index.
  ISBN 0-8061-2866-6
  1. Mayas—Guatemala—Antiquities. 2. Maya architecture—Guatemala. 3. Guatemala—Antiquities. 4. Mayas—Guatemala—Antiquities—Pictorial works. 5. Maya
architecture—Guatemala—Pictorial works. 6. Guatemala—Antiquities—Pictorial
works.
I. Bassett-VanKirk, Parney II. Title.
F1445.V36   1996
972.81'016—dc20   96-8668
                                                                                           CIP

Text design by Debora Hackworth.

1 2 3 4 5 6 7 8 9 10

To our granddaughters, Stacey Christina Segal, Abigail Castillo, Noemi Castillo, and Darrien Segal, and in memory of Commander William "Bill" Holland, Jeffery Miller, Richard Weisbrod—men who shared a love for the Maya—and of Tracey Lynn Maiers, who never got her chance.

The Maya god of writers was a monkey.
One cannot help but stand in awe
at the wisdom of the ancient ones.

CONTENTS

ix   List of Illustrations

xi   Acknowledgments

xiii   Preface

3   *The South Coast*

3   Ocos, El Jobo, and La Victoria

4   Abaj Takalik

5   Palo Gordo

5   Santa Lucía Cotzumalhuapa area

6   Monte Alto

6   Quirigua

49   *The Lowlands*

50   Canchecan

50   Naj Tunich

52   Sacul

52   Ixtutz

53   Ixkun

53   El Chal

53   Ucanal

54   Tzikin Tzakan

54   El Naranjo

54   Río Azul

57   Nakum

57   Yaxha

58   Topoxte

59   Ixlu

59   Tikal

Contents

60	Uaxactun
61	El Bejucal
61	El Zotz
62	Motul de San José
62	Tayasal
63	El Peru
64	La Florida
64	Piedras Negras
65	San Diego
65	Polol
66	Itsimte
66	Itzan
67	La Amelia
67	Dos Pilas
68	Arroyo de Piedra
68	Tamarindito
68	Aguateca
69	Cancuen
69	Tres Islas
70	Machaquila
70	Seibal
197	*The Highlands*
197	Kaminaljuyu
198	K'umarcaaj
199	Iximche
201	Zaculeu
202	Mixco Viejo
203	Maximon
237	Bibliography
239	Index

ILLUSTRATIONS

2	Map of sites in the south coast, lowlands, and highlands of Guatemala
9–48	The South Coast
73–196	The Lowlands
204–236	The Highlands

ACKNOWLEDGMENTS

It would take another book to express adequately our thanks to the people who helped make this work possible.

We were *extranjeros* in a strange land—but not for long: the people of El Peten, Los Peténeros, went a long way out of *their* way to make us feel a part of them. Even so there are some who stand apart. A very special thank-you to John McDonald, who helped get this book started. To Don Julio Godoy—one of the finest men we have met—and his warm, kind wife, Doña Linda. To Daaveed (David) Blair, our first guide and our friend. To Francisco de León, our companion for many years. To Anatolio and Manuel Perez, whom we laughed with over a lot of campfires and who taught us about El Peten. To the men who would gently take a machete from me and say, "No, Señor Van, not like that, like this." To Don Beto Gillette, the only grandfather our girls were to have. To Don Dacio Castillo, who went the extra mile for us. To Patty de Solis for bringing and keeping an elegant culture and sharing it with us. To the dozens of men who sweated our not inconsiderable amount of equipment up countless muddy banks and through many miles of steaming jungle and numberless downpours and from whom we never heard a murmur of protest!

To Professor Robert G. "Bob" Marsh, an inspiration, and to Kathlyn K. Marsh for her considerable help with words. Our deepest gratitude and affection to Jay and Sally Brandt, who went way beyond the call in giving us much-needed help when it counted. And finally, to our daughters, Gayle and Parney Lynn, "jungle rats," who helped put it all together!

PREFACE

There is very little that is new in this book. There are, however, many old things—remarkable things left behind by pre-Columbian people, mainly the Maya.

The early 1960s, when names such as Tikal and Uaxactun began appearing in magazine articles and newspapers, and, rarely, on television, ushered in a new craze: the desire to own *anything* Maya. It became a very good investment. An artifact purchased for a few dollars might be resold for thousands. Collectors were in a fever to get their hands on Maya antiquities. To people who knew nothing about them, they were an "in" thing.

Men who normally earned the equivalent of five hundred dollars or so a year soon learned that they could make many times that amount by finding Maya things. (And they *were* just lying about waiting to be picked up.) The artifact rush was on!

By a slight coincidence of history, the avaricious interest in Maya art began at about the same time as an ambitious colonization program sponsored by the Guatemalan government. Free, or almost free, land was offered to anyone who wished to settle and farm in El Peten, a region that, since the days of the ancient Maya, had remained almost entirely a vast jungle wilderness.

Pilgrims, Indians, and Ladinos alike came by the thousands. New roads were built, and towns sprang up almost overnight. The felling of the great forests of El Peten began in earnest, and in the process new discoveries came to light.

Many settlers quickly picked up on this new way of making money. *Dios mío!* Someone will pay fifty dollars for just a little clay *muñeca* (doll or figurine)?

The hunt intensified. At first it was usually an individual endeavor, undertaken by one or two men at most. The early efforts of these entrepreneurs were clumsy, often ending disastrously—pottery and vases broken, stelae shattered, cave-ins that destroyed tombs and, worse, their contents. Loners then gave way to bands of men equipped with modern tools and methods. Millions of dollars in illegal Maya artifacts began to surface in markets and collections throughout the world. Many authorities believe that profits from sales of antiquities are second only to those from drug trafficking.

Like the drug business, the antiquities trade can be dangerous. Stories abound of men buried in remote places when something went wrong in their pursuit of clay pots and jade figures.

So much Maya art appeared in the United States that the two governments signed a treaty prohibiting the transport of Maya artifacts from one country to the other. But the treaty did nothing to slow the traffic. Although the United States had shut its doors, many other countries had not. If anything, the looting intensified. Complete Maya cities were invaded. Groups of men systematically looted hundreds of ancient tombs. Planeloads of ancient Maya treasure left regularly from jungle airstrips. The authorities tried to stop the flow, but there was never enough money to finance a real effort.

With our two daughters we moved to Guatemala in the early part of the 1960s. Settling in El Peten, on a lagoon called Patixbatun, we began our new life. We built a small lodge overlooking the lagoon and started a guide service. When we were given the name of a place, we would find an Indian who knew where that place was. Many times we would see an abandoned ancient Maya site for the first time with our clients.

Soon we began to notice that sites had been damaged between our visits—often only a few months apart. At first the damage was mainly in the form of pits and the occasional clumsily contrived tunnel. But soon, newly discovered sites were being ripped up before anyone really knew anything about them.

We could say that these depredations triggered this book. They might have had something to do with it. But our main incentive was the great lost cities themselves. We wanted to record *every* Maya site in Guatemala. However, one afternoon at the Instituto de Antropología y Archeología dampened our zeal; more than five thousand sites had been recorded. We lowered our sights considerably. Our criterion became a visual one: we would photograph only those sites that were photogenic. There had to be more for the camera than a debris-covered mound.

From experience we knew that on some days the light for monuments would be good and on other days terrible. Accordingly, we acquired a six-thousand-watt generator and a good set of halogen lamps. This book is the result of several years' work in the field.

We have researched as many of the monuments as possible in regard to dedicatory dates. Of course any mistakes herein are ours alone, and we apologize for them in advance.

Finally, was it difficult? We have read many epic stories of men and women and jungles. In the nearly two decades that we lived in Guatemala—several years in the jungle—nothing untoward happened to any of us. We did encounter a few dangerous snakes and the occasional scorpion, but when we read of trees laden with the deadly fer-de-lance or of killer-bee attacks very close to where we lived, we often wondered if there were two El Petens. If we gained any expertise at all, it was with mosquitoes, gnats, fleas, flies, roaches, heat, humidity, and rain. Oh yes, and mud! We know a great deal about thick, runny, slick, viscous, slippery, cloying mud. In all colors.

We have been back in the United States now for several years. However, not a single day passes that we do not recall some friend or *compañero* left behind. And at the oddest moments names of places such as Ixcan Río, Sayaxche, and Ixkun pop unbidden into our heads.

We and our daughters, Gayle and Parney Lynn, will always have a very deep affection for Guatemala and its people.

JACQUES VANKIRK
PARNEY BASSETT-VANKIRK
Nobleton, Florida

REMARKABLE REMAINS

OF THE ANCIENT PEOPLES OF GUATEMALA

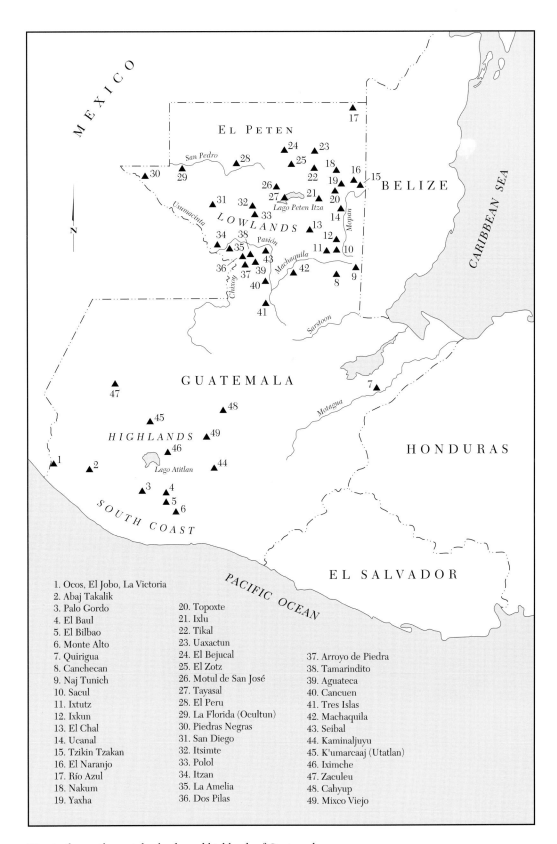

MEXICO

EL PETEN

San Pedro

BELIZE

CARIBBEAN SEA

L O W L A N D S

Usumacinta

Lago Peten Itza

Mopan

Pasión

Chixoy

Machaquila

Sarstoon

GUATEMALA

Motagua

HIGHLANDS

HONDURAS

Lago Atitlan

SOUTH COAST

EL SALVADOR

PACIFIC OCEAN

1. Ocos, El Jobo, La Victoria
2. Abaj Takalik
3. Palo Gordo
4. El Baul
5. El Bilbao
6. Monte Alto
7. Quirigua
8. Canchecan
9. Naj Tunich
10. Sacul
11. Ixtutz
12. Ixkun
13. El Chal
14. Ucanal
15. Tzikin Tzakan
16. El Naranjo
17. Río Azul
18. Nakum
19. Yaxha

20. Topoxte
21. Ixlu
22. Tikal
23. Uaxactun
24. El Bejucal
25. El Zotz
26. Motul de San José
27. Tayasal
28. El Peru
29. La Florida (Ocultun)
30. Piedras Negras
31. San Diego
32. Itsimte
33. Polol
34. Itzan
35. La Amelia
36. Dos Pilas

37. Arroyo de Piedra
38. Tamarindito
39. Aguateca
40. Cancuen
41. Tres Islas
42. Machaquila
43. Seibal
44. Kaminaljuyu
45. K'umarcaaj (Utatlan)
46. Iximche
47. Zaculeu
48. Cahyup
49. Mixco Viejo

Sites in the south coast, lowlands, and highlands of Guatemala

CHAPTER ONE

THE SOUTH COAST

OCOS, EL JOBO, AND LA VICTORIA

Two thousand years before Christ, small bands of people drifting down through Mexico began to settle on the Pacific Coast in the southwest corner of what is today Guatemala, and the Maya began their march through time.

Certainly, ease in obtaining food there became the predominant reason for settling. Aside from bounty provided by the Pacific Ocean, many lagoons and estuaries, along with freshwater rivers, teemed with fish. There was a vast variety of ducks and other water birds. Mangrove swamps provided shellfish, oysters, and clams. Flavorsome turtles could be trapped, and iguanas could easily be run down and caught. (Popularity of both turtle and iguana eggs as food has never diminished; many Guatemalans, especially men, begin their day with a glass of orange juice containing several raw turtle or iguana eggs. The latter, in particular, are thought to increase potency.)

Insofar as food and shelter were concerned, life was probably relatively untroubled for these early pioneers. Possibly there were one or two irksome things; mosquitoes, if they were as plentiful then as now, would certainly have been at the top of the list. The blazing heat of summer may have raised complaints, with temperatures that often reached over a hundred degrees. The black volcanic sands of beaches on the south coast can still absorb and hold heat from the sun to such an extent that it is nearly impossible to walk on them without some form of protection for the feet.

Usually in groups of ten or twelve, families gathered in sites that now have names such as Ocos, El Jobo, and La Victoria. Dwellings were constructed of poles, plastered with mud, and roofed with thatch. In parts of Guatemala, these types of huts are still being built in exactly the same way today. When family members died, they were buried beneath dirt floors in their homes. This custom endured for centuries throughout the land of the Maya.

As time went on, people cleared tropical forests a little higher on adjacent slopes of the Sierra Madres, a range of mountains that, like a great spine, runs the length of North and South America. (In the United States, the range is known as the Rocky Mountains.)

In cleared fields, maize (corn), squash, and beans were planted. The new farmers discovered that because of the climate and rich, fertile volcanic soil (Guatemala at present has twenty-six active volcanoes) three crops a year could be harvested. Centuries later, archaeologists in the area would discover astonishingly well-preserved maize

cobs of a variety known as Nal-Tel. After more than a thousand years, Nal-Tel is still favored by many lowland farmers.

Ocos today remains a small fishing village, and life goes on essentially the same now as it did then. Nylon has replaced hemp in nets, and outboard motors have taken the place of paddles. However, a great deal of surrounding land on the south coast has been given over to huge modern cotton, cattle, and sugarcane *fincas* (farms).

ABAJ TAKALIK (STONE PARADE)

The vast and very old Early Formative ruins of Abaj Takalik lie spread over, and under, parts of four coffee fincas and close to imaginary, yet nonetheless real, boundaries separating Mam and Quiche Maya areas of today. The site is close to the town of Retalhuleu, in the department (state) of the same name. Because of the ancient secrets that Abaj Takalik holds, it is of intense interest to archaeologists. The site, occupied through Late Classic times, contains carvings that—although difficult to interpret, often due to erosion—bear some of the earliest Maya dates known so far. The last people living at Abaj Takalik, in the Late Classic era, chose to reset the Preclassic monuments for their own use. In doing so, they added yet another layer of mystery. Archaeologist John Graham has said of Abaj Takalik, "So far, it seems as if we've excavated the New World's first museum."

Although there is certainly evidence of looting, time and a deteriorative hot, wet climate would appear to be the chief culprits of destruction at Abaj Takalik. Monuments bearing dates are so worn that interpretation is always difficult. Graham believes that he has worked out a date span for one monument of between 235 and 18 B.C., making it the oldest dated stela, by several hundred years, in the Maya area.

Abaj Takalik contains many examples of artifacts rendered in what Lee Parsons, an archaeologist who has worked in this area for many years, has labeled post-Olmec. The Olmecs were an ancient race of people that seem to have centered much farther to the west in what is now Mexico. Many scholars believe the Olmec culture to be the Mesoamerican cradle of civilization.

PALO GORDO (FAT POLE), OR PIEDRA SANTA (HOLY ROCK)

Palo Gordo, also known as Piedra Santa, is a small, early south coast site. It once contained some thirty-one human-made structures, platforms of earth faced with river-smoothed cobblestones of bowling-ball size. One of these mounds measured over eighty meters in length. Today, the entire site is covered by fields of sugarcane. When the cane is cut for harvest and before new growth appears, mounds are easily distinguishable.

SANTA LUCÍA COTZUMALHUAPA (POSSUM WATER) AREA

On our Maya march through Guatemala, we hit a little road bump in the Department of Esquintla. It seems that, although surrounded by Maya people, the Maya never occupied this area. However, some monuments found there reflect Maya influence.

Sites such as El Baul, Bilbao, Pantaleón, Las Illusiones, and El Castillo are gathered in a twenty-square-mile area—an area so small that one authority remarks that, rather than several sites, perhaps it is just one large one.

It is proposed by some that the Pipil, a tribe of people from central Mexico or southern Veracruz, were driven from their homelands by severe drought and migrated to Guatemala. Occupation at this site goes back at least to the Late Formative period, with the greatest development occurring between A.D. 650 and 925.

Many of the sculptured stones there fall in the narrative and portrait category, described by J. Eric Thompson as "pictures in stone." Death and confrontational scenes seem to reflect political turmoil for a long time before the Late Classic period.

Excavations done in the sixties revealed cobblestone streets, drainage systems, and a twenty-five-foot stone bridge that employed the famed Maya corbeled arch. Mounds that supported temples made from perishable material were faced with smooth river stones. Although there have been more than two hundred large stone monuments recorded in the area, only six remain in situ. The mounds, covered by sugarcane, are still visible.

Traffic in artifacts is a way of life around Cotzumalhuapa, and has been for a long time. In 1876 a German named Carl Herman Berendt excavated, lightened by cutting away excess stone, and shipped to Germany no fewer than thirty major monuments along with several minor ones. Berendt claimed to have found most of the monuments "in a jumble of half buried stone sculptures called the mine." The mine area has since been renamed Monument Plaza. It took the hardworking Berendt over five years to complete his project, and, as can be imagined, the going was not always smooth. One great monument, for example, fell into the water as it was being loaded aboard ship at Puerto Barrios and was never recovered.

At least two more monuments were victims of World War II. Germany, desperate for building materials to restore structures damaged by Allied bombers attacking Berlin, replaced the sides of a Berlin doorway with two carved basalt columns from Berendt's excavations. Cemented over, their present location is not known.

Sugarcane covers most mounds at Cotzumalhuapa now, but in the distant past cacao, the currency of the times, was the most important cultivated crop. In 1819 an archaeologist was told by an Indian that one monument he inquired about was the god of cacao.

MONTE ALTO (HIGH BUSH)
Few sites have elicited as much controversy as that of Monte Alto. Many claimed—some still do—that the site is pre-Olmec and, in reality, the origin of New World civilization. In 1968 a team of investigators determined that the eleven massive monuments (some weighing up to sixteen tons) that were found there, placed in a row, were all carved between the time of Christ and three hundred years earlier. It was noticed recently that four of the huge figures had some sort of magnetic attraction located in their heads. A question immediately arose: Could the Maya determine directions magnetically?

Boulder sculptures in the forms of heads, fat boys, and potbellied figures like those found at Monte Alto are common on the entire coastline, ranging from Mexico south into Guatemala and El Salvador. No one has yet determined the real purpose of these strange figures. One authority says that they may be simply a fat god, without known functions. The large number of potbellied figures and large heads found in Mesoamerica attests to the fact that whomever they represented, they were *very* important.

Almost nothing remains at the original site of Monte Alto. The huge figures have been transported—and that was a job—to the nearby town of La Democracia, where they are arranged around the town plaza, nicely surrounded by tropical flowers.

QUIRIGUA
Although separated from El Peten, the heart of the lowland Maya, by mountains—the Sierra de Las Minas and, beyond Lago Izabal, the Sierra de Santa Cruz—Quirigua is still classified as a lowland site.

In the eastern part of Guatemala, not far from the present-day border of Honduras, is one of the loveliest jewels in the Maya crown, Quirigua. The small site is located in the incredibly fertile Motagua valley, floodplain for the Motagua River. Once again, rich land probably attracted early settlers. Today, Quirigua is surrounded by miles of banana plantations. There are archaeological data pointing to the possibility that the site was founded by a group related to the dynasties of Tikal.

Quirigua was one of the last lowland Maya centers to collapse, living on beyond the ninth century. Control over an important trade route, the Motagua River, may have been a prime reason for the site's longevity. Also, Quirigua lay in the heart of the cacao-growing area, and cacao beans were the currency of the land.

Restored mainly by the United Fruit Company in the early 1900s, Quirigua has no imposing great structures like those found at Tikal or Mirador. The site is, however, renowned for its elegantly carved stelae.

In the year A.D. 742 a king called Cauac Sky rose to power, reigning for more than fifty years. Every five years during his rule, monuments were dedicated to Cauac Sky. Of the sixteen great monuments discovered at Quirigua, ten were erected while Cauac Sky ruled and at least one more is associated with him.

It appears that Quirigua was, for awhile, a satellite or client state of the great Maya center Copan, which lies some thirty miles to the south just across the border of present-day Honduras. It seems that on the day of May 1, A.D. 738—the date appears on several Quirigua stelae—Cauac Sky captured the ruler of Copan in battle and killed him by beheading. From that time until its collapse, Quirigua was on its own.

What cannot be photographed or recorded, nor indeed captured in any way other than by one's actual presence, is the ambience of this lovely site. Early morning ground mists, the trilling of myriad birds and flashes of their brilliant colors as they fly about, the tropical fragrance, and the almost tangible presence of a bygone greatness combine to flood the senses as one walks among the towering reminders of a past glory.

A small, worn stela from Abaj Takalik, one of the oldest known Maya sites. Hieroglyphs on stelae found there are so badly damaged that rendering absolute dates has been impossible. Many scientists believe the south coast is the cultural doorway to the Lowland Maya, through which passed the stelae cult, hieroglyphics, calendrics, mathematics, and, perhaps, astronomy.

This strange artifact was recovered from Abaj Takalik. The bird perched on top is possibly a macaw or an owl; the animal at the bottom is probably a deer. The purpose this stone served for the Maya may never be known.

Crudely carved into a stone boulder at Abaj Takalik, the figure in this petroglyph sits at an altar.
Designated as Monument 1, it is very old, perhaps going back to post-Olmec times.

Above: *El gorobo* (the iguana) is a tropical American lizard that can grow to a length of over six feet. The animal, prized for its purported medicinal properties as well as for food, is commonly sold live at markets throughout Guatemala.

Below: A small stela from Palo Gordo, featuring a carved iguana. Itzam Na, the most powerful god in the Maya pantheon, is often represented as an iguana, lizard, or crocodile manifestation.

11

This well-preserved stone once served as an altar
at the site of Piedra Santa.

Stela 1 (also known as the Herrera Stela), is a very early dated monument in the Maya area. Despite badly damaged and missing hieroglyphs, it has been placed as early as A.D. 36. Stela 1 stood until recently in front of a mound that contained several monuments held sacred by Indians today. Supplicants on their way to worship these monuments would ask permission to pass from the figure on the stone, referring to it as El Guardian. They would often build offertory fires at the base of the carving, which, over the years, caused the stone to flake away. It was for this reason that the monument was finally transported to finca headquarters at El Baul.

Unearthed by plows in 1964, Stela 27 was discovered just a few inches below the surface of the ground. As it was in perfect condition, it was decided to reerect the monument on the spot. Soon, however, the Indians began building their usual offertory fires at the base of the stela. Alert finca managers quickly moved the deeply carved monument to headquarters at El Baul, where it would be safe from further damage.

Above: A jaguar/reptile monster, Monument 26, crouches among several other stone carvings at Finca El Baul headquarters.

Below: Larger than life, this great stone jaguar once guarded the front of a temple at El Baul. Such monuments with no hieroglyphs are difficult to date, but Mayanist Eric Thompson declared no monument at El Baul was carved later than A.D. 900.

Above: Many of the carvings found in the Cotzumalhuapa area show a marked concern with death. Here, a fanged snake, most likely the feared *barba amarilla* (or fer-de-lance), emerges from a human skull. This monument is also at El Baul.

Below: Now a great sugar-producing area, Cotzumalhaupa was once the center for cacao growing in Guatemala. This figure with its great headdress was referred to by the Indians as the god of cacao.

16

Monument 4 is the only basalt boulder carving found at El Baul. A tall figure wearing a death mask holds aloft a heart just removed from a sacrificial victim; other victims surround him, with chests torn open and heads cut off. The central figure displays a heavily calloused left knee, identifying him as a ballplayer. Cacao pods and vines wend their way through the carving's design. The massive stone is three meters wide and three and one-half meters tall.

One of the most impressive carvings at El Baul is Monument 3, which is also one of the most sacred to the Indians. Sitting massively on top of a mound, the great stone, by its sheer weight, is causing the monument to sink gradually into the earth. The stone head has many names among its adorados; King of the Quiches, God of the Earth, Tecun Uman, God, and Jesus are but a few. Supplicants offer candles, pom, sugar, rum, food, and sometimes money to the great head. Shamans and *curanderos* (Indian priests who heal the sick) bring afflicted and sick people there, entreating help from the stone. A Bible is often used—mixed with non-Christian rites—in prayers to the colossal head. Ceremonies, including symbolic flagellation in expiation of sins, are sometimes enacted in front of the idol. Countless offertory fires have caused the nose to begin flaking away.

Located about thirty meters across the top of the mound from El Dios del Mundo, Monument 2 at El Baul is also sacred to Indian worshipers. Because of its dresslike raiment, the idol is referred to as feminine, usually as the Queen of the Quiches or the Virgin Mary. An offering of sugar has been sprinkled over the idol here. Offertory fires have damaged the lower part of the ancient carving.

In the midst of sugarcane fields that now cover even the palace mounds, several monuments lie exposed at the ruins of Bilbao, a site close to El Baul on the south coast. This stone shows two confronting figures, the one on the left definitely in better shape. Archaeologist Lee Parsons has suggested that the anthropomorphic bird and jaguar appearing behind the figures are their alter egos, and may also have represented military orders found in central Mexico. Because of its raiment and hairstyle, the figure on the left might be that of a woman. Ceramic pottery excavated from beneath the boulder showed that it was set in place no later than 700 to 930 A.D. The dots across the center of the boulder are holes left by drills when thieves tried to break the monument up into pieces that would be easier to carry. The culprits were apprehended in time to save the monument.

20

Many consider Monument 21 at Bilbao the finest carving ever done by pre-Columbian people. Over three meters across, the stone is covered with deep relief carvings. The center figure seems to be handing a cacao pod that he has just cut from a vine to the man seated on a throne and adorned with a nose bone. Beneath the throne are other items of tribute that the seated figure appears to have accepted. To the left, a smaller figure gestures with a conjurer's bone in one hand while manipulating a hand puppet in the other. His attitude is one of marked unfriendliness toward the seated man. Notice the extremely calloused knee of the central figure, the mark of a ballplayer. Monument 21 has been assigned a date of A.D. 527.

Confronting figures is a common theme at Bilbao, repeated here on Monument 18. The artist has exaggerated the kneecaps of the central and right-hand figures. Several carved figures on stones in the area have feet turned sideways—as Eric Thompson pointed out, "almost as if they wanted to prove they had ten toes."

Above: Knowing of the existence of a small carved offertory basin at Bilbao but unable to locate it, I hired a group of young Indian boys to cut away tall grass and weeds about where the monument known as Los Gemelas (The Twins) was supposed to be. Eventually the boys uncovered the small stone, and it was discovered that *new* holes had been drilled in the head of one of the figures. The purpose of the holes remains a mystery. This artifact was once used as a receptacle for hearts from sacrificed victims. A blood groove had been cut into one side of the basin.

Below: This strange anthropomorphic figure has been called the Crab God. It is in a private collection.

Standing just over two feet tall, this stela greets visitors at the entrance to a driveway on a south coast finca.

This wonderfully contrived portrait in stone of a noble face causes the visitor at Finca San Francisco to pause and wonder just who and what he was.

At the site of Pantaleón on Finca el Castillo, several monuments and artifacts have been brought in from the fields where they were discovered. On display in the front yard of finca headquarters stands a rare type of stela. The monument is carved on both sides, but in two very different styles. On this side, a figure climbs a ladder toward what appears to be the sun god.

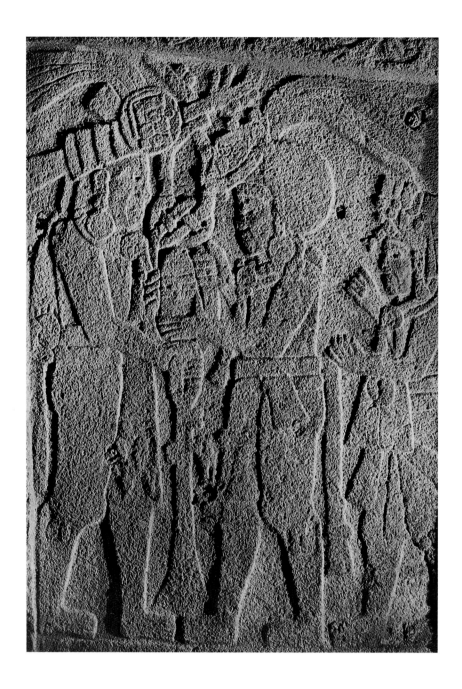

The reverse side of Monument 1 at Pantaleón features confronting figures with exaggerated calloused kneecaps. In the Mesoamerican ball game the usual object of the game (fifteen versions are known to have been played) seems to have been to keep the ball from hitting the ground on one's own side. Players were not allowed to use their hands to hit the ball but could use their elbows, chests, heads, and hips. In order to keep from being scored upon, players often threw themselves to their knees, diving for low balls. Since evidence exists that sometimes the losers were decapitated, it might be assumed that participants gave the game their all, which likely accounts for scarred and calloused knees.

The theme of humans appearing to emerge, perhaps being born, from the mouths of serpent monsters was a favorite of pre-Columbian artists throughout the Maya area.

One of the most bizarre-appearing forms of stone sculpture from the south coast features a face with one or both eyes extruded from their sockets. This portrayal is common in Mexican art and usually symbolizes weeping, particularly penitent weeping. Eric Thompson thought such figures could represent the Mexican god Nanahuatl (The Syphilitic One), credited with introducing penitential bloodletting. It is the god Ehecatl, the wind god, however, who is most represented in this form. The profusion of this distinctive representation once led to the theory that people of the south coast may have been afflicted with some form of eye disease at one time.

Above: Not far from Pantaleón, at Hacienda El Cerritos, stands this mysterious stela. Sometime in the past, the monument was lowered and a tenon was fashioned at its base. The great stone was then set into a wall, where it acted as a table. The deep groove was carved into the figures at that time. I believe it was then used as a sacrificial table, the groove used to carry away blood from the victims.

Opposite above: Another of the colossal stone heads discovered at Monte Alto. All of the monuments from the site are now on display at the La Democrácia town square and museum. Interestingly, it was recently found that several of the monuments exhibited magnetic attractions. No one knows what this might mean. Most scientists dismiss the claim as unimportant.

Below: For a time after the 1938 discovery of several fat boy figures at Finca Monte Alto on the south coast, it was thought that, because of their style, they were pre-Olmec. When several more of these monolithic boulders were found at the same site in 1968, a team of scientists led by Edwin Shook investigated and determined that the monuments had been carved between the time of Christ and three hundred years before. The effigies are all carved with figures and faces that conform to the natural shapes of the basalt boulders. Some of the boulders weigh up to sixteen tons.

The artist who created this clay face managed to convey an almost uncanny human quality. So great were the number of clay artifacts such as bowls, figures, vases, and funeraries left behind by the Maya that it is said one merely has to scratch the ground in Guatemala to find something. This piece is from Tiquisate, a town on the south coast.

The remains of a clay effigy discovered on the south coast. Few homes in this area are without collections of antiquities, and many of the private collections are extensive. Private ownership of artifacts that are legitimately found on one's property is not against the law. Selling them for transportation out of the country is.

The carved back of Stela I at Quirigua. The stone bears a date of A.D. 800. The carved panels of brown sandstone stand over thirteen feet tall. The front of Stela I bears the likeness of Cauac Sky.

Altar L is the smallest monument to have been found at Quirigua. Just over three feet wide and less than a foot thick, the stone bears what has been called a questionable date of A.D. 725. Because of the relative ease with which this small monument could be moved, it was decided to bring it to the National Museum in Guatemala City for protection.

Left: Stela J was the first stela at Quirigua on which head-variant hieroglyphs were used for numbers, instead of the usual bar-and-dot system. Stela J (shown here from the back), which commemorates the end of a five-year period, is dated at A.D. 756. The top of its carved portion stands nearly seventeen feet high.

Right: Immortalized in stone. Cauac Sky, on Stela K, has stood for over a thousand years at Quirigua.

Above: Like giant anthills, mounds that once supported Maya structures dot the vast sprawling cotton fields of the south coast. As the fields are prepared for new planting each year, the great plows chew off a few more feet of the mounds.

Below: Life on the Pacific Coast is much the same today as it was in ancient times. Outboard motors have replaced paddles and nets are now made of nylon, but fishermen still live in thatch-roofed huts, still dry and repair fishnets and traps, and make their living from the sea.

Parney VanKirk examines one of the so-called fat boy figures found throughout the south coast. This one sits in a small clearing among coffee trees at Abaj Takalik.

This small stela from the site of Palo Gordo shows a figure wearing the chest girdle of a ballplayer. The stone has been reerected in the school yard of the town. Palo Gordo is also known as Piedra Santa (Holy Stone) by local people.

35

Opposite: Seated along the railroad tracks that run through the site of Palo Gordo is the hulking figure known as Piedra Santa, which is worshipped as a god. *Adorados* offer pom, flowers, sugar, candles, and other gifts. (Pom is an incense that is made from the gum of a pine tree. It has been found in the identical form in which it is used today in tombs thousands of years old.) The huge idol, described as an anthropomorphic jaguar monster, could date back to as early as 350 to 100 B.C. The figure was carved from a four-ton block of granite. The prominent snout on Piedra Santa was knocked off by missionaries in the sixteenth century in an attempt to destroy the idol.

Above: In the south coast area of Santa Lucía Cotzumalhuapa, over two hundred monuments have been discovered. More are found each year as the great sugarcane fields covering the sites are prepared for planting. For a brief time, after the mature sugarcane has been harvested, the outlines of palaces and temples can be seen.

Cacao beans, once the coin of the Maya realm. Ground into powder, mixed with maize flour, and added to water, cacao, served hot and frothy, was highly prized by the Maya elite. The beans were traded throughout Guatemala. At the time of the Spanish conquest, they were valued at one gold peso, or *escudo*, per four thousand beans—in today's money, about sixty dollars. Much cheaper now, the same number of cacao beans would bring about twenty dollars. At one time, a very long time ago, a Maya who possessed cacao could get for his beans, among other things: one rabbit or eight pieces of a local fruit called *chico zapote*; a slave for around one hundred beans; and the services of a *gutepol* (prostitute) for eight or ten beans.

It was around this time that perhaps the first counterfeiting in the Americas took place. The sixteenth-century historian Gonzalo Fernández de Oviedo y Valdés wrote:

And even in that almond money cacao beans one finds falsification in order that one may cheat the other and mix the fake pieces among a quantity of good ones. These false pieces are made by removing the bark or skin which some of the beans have, just like our almonds, and fill[ing] them with earth or something similar, and they close the hole with such skill that one cannot see it. In order to beware of this falsification, he who receives the almonds must revise them one by one when he counts them, and place his first finger of the next one against his thumb, pressing each almond, because even though a false one is well filled it can be felt by the touch to be different from the real ones.

An elderly Quiche Indian prepares his offerings
to the God of the Earth. He will burn candles and
pom as offerings to aid him in his prayers. When
later asked what he had prayed for, the old gen-
tleman replied, "I have a granddaughter who is
sick. El Dios del Mundo will make her better."

Opposite: So common are artifacts on the south coast that very few fincas in the area are without some sort of ancient stonework adorning driveways, frontyards, or patios. This large monkey head, with a fresh coat of paint, graces the entrance to one such finca.

Above: Confronting heads. This carving is from a private collection. The same two figures are depicted on the great Monument 21. On both stones, the figure with the nose bone has a rattlesnake entwined in his headdress on both stones.

Below: At the headquarters of Finca San Francisco, a short distance from El Baul and Bilbao, a collection of stone artifacts has been placed on display. A goggle-eyed visage of the Mexican rain god, Tlaloc, has been erected in the patio.

Above: This large jade mask, whose owner wishes to remain anonymous, is from a private collection in Guatemala. The Olmec-style mask is nearly seven inches in height and weighs several pounds. The owner stated that this piece, and that in the following illustration, were brought to him by an itinerant worker at his south coast finca.

Opposite: Jade was highly prized by the Maya. Artisans used simple tools such as bird-bone drills dipped in pulverized jade powder, along with cord saturated with animal fat that was covered with abrasive jade dust and used as a saw, to cut the extremely hard jade. Months would be spent fashioning the green stone into incredibly intricate pieces of art. Such a piece is this Olmec figure, privately owned and reported to have come from the south coast.

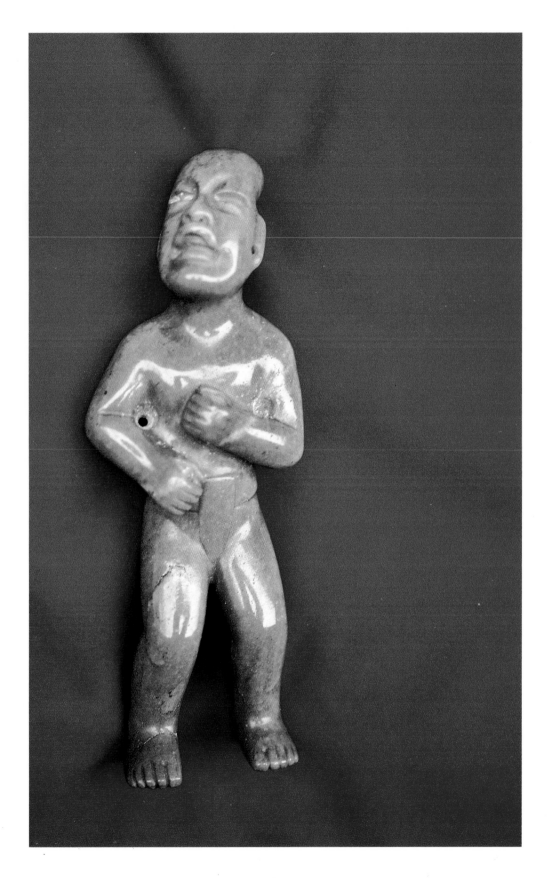

Above: Zoomorphs at Quirigua, which resemble huge, sometimes toadlike monsters, are among the most intricate carvings done by Maya craftspeople. Zoomorph P is the largest and most elaborate such monument at Quirigua. Carved from brown sandstone, this massive monument bears a dedicatory date of A.D. 795. It was the last of several zoomorphs carved at Quirigua.

Opposite: Quirigua's Stela E not only commemorates a great ruler, Cauac Sky, but stands as a silent tribute to the engineering skills of the ancient Maya. The sandstone shaft is thirty-five feet in length, over four feet thick, and weighs more than sixty-five tons. In what certainly must have been a herculean task—the Maya had no wheel—the huge stone was transported several miles from where it was quarried, set in place, and carved. The date on Stela E is A.D. 771. The monument marks the end of a five-year period, or hotun. This is the largest single block of stone ever quarried by the Maya.

Above: Birds and their songs are one of the many attractions that draw visitors to Quirigua. One of the most colorful birds is the mot-mot. A first sighting usually gives the impression that the bird has had an accident that has damaged its tail feathers, leaving them with a tennis-racket appearance, but this is a normal condition. An Indian legend tells how it came about. When the earth was being created, the lord enlisted the help of the animals. All of them happily complied except the mot-mot, who spent her days preening and exclaiming how beautiful she was. The lord eventually lost his patience, grabbed the mot-mot, and stripped away a considerable portion of her tail feathers, and the bird has been that way ever since.

Opposite: Two variant date glyphs from the text on Stela D. It has long been known that the Maya had an overwhelming preoccupation with the passage of time. Two stelae at Quirigua, J and D, bear dates that mark specific days 90 million and 400 million years in the past.

An almost immediate attempt was made to steal
a large mask of the Maya sun god, Kinich Ahau,
when it was unearthed at Quirigua by excavators
from the University of Pennsylvania in 1975. As
a result, it is no longer on display but is safely
stored in a government warehouse.

Chapter Two

THE LOWLANDS

The Lowlands, or El Peten (The Island)

Chicleros, the men who gather sap from the chicle tree for chewing gum, have, in their quest for the trees, traveled throughout the jungles of El Peten. They have been given rightful credit for many grand Maya discoveries. With the advent of artificial chewing gum, ever fewer men opted for careers in the gum-gathering business. As the searchers declined, so did discoveries, until the modern colonization program for El Peten began. Centuries before, El Peten had been home to the vast majority of Maya. Some estimates place the number of Maya that lived there in excess of three million. Abandoned for the most part before the ninth century, it was for a long time a vast wilderness.

When the Guatemalan government began opening up El Peten for modern colonization by building roads and promising free—or very inexpensive—land, thousands of land-hungry people from all over Guatemala poured into El Peten. Clearing land by slashing and burning, the same method used by their ancestors on the same land more than a thousand years before, the people turned up ancient sites and sacred places by the dozens. Frequently, new towns were built on ancient sites. Sadly, most, if not all, were looted before their locations became known to proper authorities. We know of one or two occasions on which the authorities were, in fact, the chief culprits.

CANCHECAN

A cleared *milpa* (cornfield) in a wide spot in the road just outside Poptun, know locally as Canchecan, revealed a grotto beneath an overhang in a limestone outcropping. Several tombs, thoroughly looted, had human faces, or perhaps skulls, carved in the walls above the tombs. Bodies had been laid out in holes scooped in the earth, but the graves were so badly torn up that nothing else could be made of them. Broken pottery literally covered the surrounding floor.

NAJ TUNICH (STONE HOUSE)

The Maya Mountains comprise the eastern border of the Maya lowlands of El Peten. They present some of the most formidable terrain in Guatemala to the traveler. This newly formed range is steep, sharp, jagged, and choked with jungle growth. The few trails entering the mountains pass between hills and ridges that often act as catchments for rain, forming sinkholes and bogs of mud; shielded from the sun by the dense canopy, they never really dry out. This wild upheaval, with its tumblings and upthrustings of limestone, con-

tains dozens of caves, caverns, and natural tunnels, twisting their convoluted way into the bowels of the earth.

Occasionally, a traveler in this area emerges momentarily from the dark forest into one of the small, fertile green valleys. Often these more favorable places are homes for Indian families, eking out a living almost exactly as their ancestors did.

In a valley such as this, close to what is now the border between Guatemala and Belize, lives a Kekchi Maya Indian by the name of Emilio Pop. After spending several days with Don Emilio, I came to know him as a warm, open, but very humble man.

One day in 1978, Emilio was hunting in the surrounding jungle close to his home. His luck that day was astounding. A *coche* (wild peccary) was flushed by his dogs. Emilio shot hastily, only wounding the animal, which raced away through the undergrowth. Tracked by the hunter and his excited dogs, the spoor led to the mouth of a huge cavern. Emilio Pop followed the beast into a tremendous opening in the earth and made a great discovery.

The yawning mouth of Naj Tunich opens into an immense cavern some ninety feet wide and four hundred and fifty feet long. The floor in this first cavern is of dirt and reasonably level. A wall of natural boulders, abetted by masonry, stands at one end. The Maya had constructed several stone tombs, which had since been broken into, on top of the wall. A small passageway led from this balcony opening into what is now called the Grand Concourse, a somewhat level passage that continues for over fifteen hundred feet before forking into two branches.

Along the way, about one hundred and forty feet into the Grand Concourse, one encounters a *nacimiento* (spring) and pool of water in the path. The depth of the pool varies considerably with the seasons, being full during the rains and nearly dry, except for the continuous spring, in the dry season. Water from caves was very important to the Maya. They believed—as they do today—that tricklings from stalactites deep in caves produce the purest of water, necessary for use in certain religious rites. The exclusion of women from these holy places because of supposed contamination was a rigidly enforced priestly law. Among the Maya today, women are still prohibited from entering caves that contain water. It is in the two forks of the cave that all but two of the fantastic Maya paintings at Naj Tunich were discovered.

I first learned of the existence of the cave in May 1980, from a friend living in Poptun. Emilio had deliberately kept the discovery of his find a secret, claiming later that he was afraid of what might happen to him once the cave was known about. I suspect, after talking with him, that perhaps respect or fear of ancient gods, still worshiped, may have had something to do with Emilio's reluctance. Also, Emilio's son, Barnabé Pop, a rather sophisticated young ex-Guatemalan soldier far more worldly than his father, may have had his own motives for keeping secrets. On two successive trips into Naj Tunich, Barnabé privately offered me artifacts that he said he had found, denying that they had come from the cave.

On our first excursion to Naj Tunich, sherds of polychrome pottery lay about, particularly near the tombs. The pieces appeared to be nearly all there. When reassembled by an expert, the artifacts would have fetched quite a bit of money from collectors. Our party touched nothing, leaving the sherds exactly as we found them. On my second trip, some months later, no trace of the pottery remained.

The paintings of Naj Tunich, on the smooth walls that had once contained an underground river, have been called the greatest Maya archaeological discovery in a quarter century. They have been likened to the discovery of a codex, a Maya book of extreme rarity. (Several codices have been found throughout the Maya area, but only three and a portion of another were in a condition to be studied. Others have pages stuck together or have been so badly decayed that it has been impossible to interpret them.)

In all, Naj Tunich contained ninety drawings, forty-four of which depicted human figures; forty-seven hieroglyphic texts included some five hundred hieroglyphs. Unfortunately, what is surely one of the greatest archaeological losses ever has occurred at Naj Tunich. In spite of protective measures, including guards and an iron gate, desecraters broke into the cave sometime in the early 1990s and destroyed or damaged twenty-three of the priceless drawings. There was a portent that something of the kind might happen when, in 1986, thieves broke the lock on the gate and dug several pits in the hopes of finding something of value. After that, security was said to have been tightened.

Archaeologist James Brady, the first to conduct scientific research at Naj Tunich, had the unhappy task of reporting, "In some cases, mud was smeared across drawings; others were scratched or struck with a hard object. Some were wiped completely off walls." Brady reported that there were no evident signs of attempted looting during the senseless attack. The Guatemalan authorities have since tightened security again at the site. Brady sadly relates, "Archaeologists who work for years at a site form a bond with it that is intense and personal. For me the job of checking the inscriptions, drawing by drawing, was like conducting an inquest for a murdered friend."

Who did it? No one knows for sure; however, I have my own thoughts about the tragedy. The first notice of the existence of Naj Tunich (at the time yet unnamed) came to light in August 1980. *Prensa Libre*, the national newspaper of Guatemala, published a front-page, headlined article, accompanied by several photographs of Naj Tunich that we had provided. Hundreds of Indians from throughout Guatemala began making pilgrimages to the site. Naj Tunich became, once again, a holy place. I think that a group of religious fanatics, perhaps sickened and angered by thoughts that some of the people were returning to old, pagan

ways (many had never left), made a trip to the cave on a dark night, broke the lock on the protective gate, and, by the light of flashlights, zealously desecrated what had once again become sacred to the Maya.

I do not like caves. Thoughts of tons of rock overhead, mud and dampness, tight spots one sometimes has to squirm through, and incredible spelaean blackness combine to trigger within me a great deal of unease. Yet, standing in front of a painting or panel of hieroglyphic text where no one else has been for a thousand years or more certainly brought about a buoyancy of spirit that, at least in my lifetime, is unsurpassed.

SACUL

Sacul is a Classic to Late Classic Maya center situated in the splendid Mopan valley a little north of Poptun and close by the Mopan River.

There were ten Stelae discovered there. The fragments of two of them are left at the site, and, on our visit, these were crated for shipment to somewhere safe. The quality of stonework can be seen in the remains of a stairway still in place. All that remains of thirty-four original buildings at the site are grass-covered mounds. No restoration has been attempted thus far. The site has been cleared, and is kept that way by *guardianes* (park guards).

IXTUTZ

The ruins at Ixtutz are in five groups. Three of these groups are connected by *calzados* (causeways). Low, earthen pyramids once supported structures constructed of perishable materials that have decayed. Often, holes left by poles that held walls in place are still in evidence. Very similar to stairways in the relatively close ruins of Sacul, several stairways of well-dressed limestone at Ixtutz remain in situ. No stelae survive at Ixtutz; anything considered valuable has been either stolen or removed by authorities to a safer place.

IXKUN (HOUSE OF GOD)

Ixkun consists of an artificially constructed acropolis on top of which pyramids, temples, and courts had been erected. Standing in the midst of the ruins—now only nondescript, debris-covered mounds—is Stela 1, the tallest monument (just short of four meters) of any found in El Peten so far. The carving on Stela 1 is exceptional and well preserved. The monolith features four figures, two confronting each other and two who are bound prisoners. The faces on all four figures are very expressive.

The text holds an error in its dedication date, which was discovered by Teobert Maler, an archaeologist visiting the site in the early part of the century. By mathematical sleuthing he worked out seven possibilities, finally choosing October 9, A.D. 790, as the correct date for the monument. He based his decision on the theory that "such is the aesthetic merit of Stela 1, that it could have been executed only during the great period." Two other period markers mentioned by Maler are no longer in evidence at the site.

Given the end result of mistakes made by scribes and others (many authorities believe the culprit wound up a sacrificial victim as punishment for errors committed), one cannot help but wonder at the apparent sloppiness, both carved in stone and painted on walls, that evidently occurred. There are at least a dozen or so impossible dates that have been found so far in El Peten alone.

A trail of about six kilometers leads from the town of Dolores north of Poptun, on the Poptun to Flores road, to the ruins of Ixkun.

EL CHAL

Actually built on top of an ancient Maya center, the new town of El Chal sits astride the road a few miles north of Poptun. Cornfields covering most of the site and a destructive climate have not been kind to the limestone stelae and altars. There are many holes dug at various points in town, signs left by hopeful residents. If a painted vase or pot is unearthed, a man can sell it for many times what he would normally make in a year's work.

UCANAL (THE PLACE OF THE UCAN TREES)

A small monument of debris-covered mounds at Ucanal supports theories of Mexican invasion or, at least, considerable Mexican influence.

Ucanal lies on the midline of El Peten, near the present border of Belize.

One archaeologist referred to the site as Yokanal. He claims that the name derives from Joe Channel, an old mahogany camp, long deserted, that lay nearby. The name, he says, was corrupted by woodcutters from nearby Belize (then known as British Honduras) into Yokanal.

TZIKIN TZAKAN

Until early 1980, a building standing at the ruins of Tzikin Tzakan was perhaps the longest of its kind ever discovered in Guatemala. The palace was over one hundred and thirty feet long and approximately forty feet wide. Two corbeled chambers ran the length of the structure, divided by a nine-foot-thick center wall. Three wide doorways, with wooden lintels intact, led into the palace, and three more on the interior led to the second long chamber. The first chamber had collapsed sometime in the past.

We first saw this great building with its wonderful arches in February 1980. During a second trip there just four months later, we found the second chamber also lay in complete ruin, having fallen in upon itself. The rainy seasons of 1979 and 1980 were particularly heavy, and there is little doubt that this was a major factor in the destruction.

Apart from the remains of this building and several debris-choked mounds, we found nothing else. No stelae, not even fragments, were apparent. The site had long since been systematically looted.

This small Late Classic site lies just off the road and up a steep hill, about ten kilometers from Belize near the town of Melchoir de Mencos.

EL NARANJO (THE ORANGE)

From 1905, the year of its discovery, until there was nothing left to steal, this site has been a looter's paradise. Shattered remains of stelae and altars—some destroyed by air drills—are scattered throughout the site.

To say that nothing of interest remains at El Naranjo is both true and untrue. For the tourist and casual student of the Maya, there *isn't* much: the great temples have fallen, and pyramids and palaces have been overtaken and buried beneath centuries of jungle growth. On the other hand, not much excavation (except by looters) has been carried out. Of the forty stelae recorded at El Naranjo, only one remains at the site; uncarved, it is considered worthless by looters. This ancient Maya center should be very rewarding for future archaeologists.

Fortunately, and mostly due to the efforts of archaeologist/explorer Ian Graham, several monuments from the site have been transported to the border town of Melchor de Mencos, where some of them have been reerected.

El Naranjo lies about fifteen kilometers northwest of Melchor and can be reached by an old lumber road that leads to the site. Accessibility is entirely controlled by weather. A one-hour rain can turn the road into a quagmire. It took us three separate visits before we made it, and that was in the heart of the dry season.

RÍO AZUL (BLUE RIVER)

Fifty miles north of Tikal, just a few miles from the borders of both Mexico and Belize in Guatemala's northeast corner, are the ruins of Río Azul, named for the nearby river. The time span for this great site runs from Preclassic through Late Classic times. The site is just a mile or so from one of the largest chicle camps in the Peten, Ixkan Río, serving the chicle gatherers from all three countries. It is there that hundreds of men bring the sap of the chicle tree to be boiled down and later flown out from the nearby airfield of Dos Lagunas.

Scholars have determined that Río Azul was a special center for the Maya, of particular military importance. The function of the rulers of Río Azul was evidently to oversee and secure part of the northern frontier, offering protection and probably exacting taxes on an important trade route.

On a visit to our very good friend, frequent companion, and guide Don Anatolio Lopez, in Flores, Peten, a very excited "Nacho" advised us to "drop everything" and come with him to visit a site where, according to him, looters had been caught in the act by the police just a week previously. There had been a gun battle; according to Nacho, two of the looters had been wounded but had managed to escape into the surrounding jungle.

Nacho advised us to rent a jeep powered by a motorcycle engine, "a little one, something we can lift over logs and so on." Despite the ominous sound of the word *lift,* we did as Nacho asked; packed solidly with tents, lights, cameras, and generator, we set off. The trip took over ten hours. We had some de-

cent roads, thanks to the lumber and oil companies, but there were enough *berechas* (unimproved jungle trails) to keep one awake at the wheel. There was some lifting and clearing of fallen trees with machetes. Parney, unable to sit, rode the entire time *crouched* over the generator in a tiny space behind our seats. She was to say later that the uncomfortable position, the heat and smell of gasoline, and the terrible jouncing she endured made the trip a nightmare. She made not the slightest protest, however, going or coming.

We spent the night at the chicle camp, and the next morning drove the few kilometers to the parking lot that the guardianes had cut out of the bush. We walked among tall temples with roof combs thrusting up out of the jungle canopy. One could not help noticing the tunnels that had been opened into these structures.

Nacho had continually rattled on excitedly about something he would show us. "Una cosa muy preciosa," was the way he put it, something he was sure we had never seen before. He was right.

He led us to a tunnel that looked terribly uninviting—cut into the side of one of the temples—and ushered us in. Several feet within, at the end of the passageway, we came upon a small hole in the floor. I rigged Parney with a rope and lowered her into the blackness with a flashlight. Her immediate yelps and cries alarmed me. (She is not the yelping kind.) I began hauling her out, but she resisted, finally making it clear to me that she was all right but surrounded by an incredible scene. When I had worked my way through the small opening that had been opened by looters into what was a tomb, I was stunned.

The walls of the ancient crypt were covered with paintings. Over a coating of creamy white, ancient scribes had left their messages in black and red. The floor was bare; even the bones of the entombed noble had been tossed out. But by a stroke of exceptional luck, the *guecheros* (grave robbers) had broken in at the only possible place that would not damage the murals— through the roof.

The date contained in the hieroglyphic inscriptions was September 29, A.D. 416. Scholars would later determine that this was the birthdate of the noble interred in the lavish tomb.

As we spent the day setting lights and photographing panels, I could not help thinking: If the ancient Maya had not expected anyone to open these tombs, who were the messages for? The answer, of course, had to be their gods. Or were these carefully painted murals for the benefit of those left behind, reassuring them that the man they were about to entomb had been very important?

Archaeologists have determined that Río Azul was abandoned around A.D. 535. The site was reoccupied sometime later and finally overrun circa A.D. 830. It was to be overrun again in our times, in the sixties, seventies, and eighties.

Several years after our visit in 1981, Archaeologist R. E. W. Adams led teams of researchers in excavating and mapping Río Azul. Their research would turn up appalling facts. They discovered more than one hundred and fifty unauthorized human-made tunnels. Thirty-two tombs had been thoroughly sacked. In Adams's words: "We have an idea of how the depredations program at Río Azul was run. Workers were recruited locally, and an effort was made to get those who had had previous archaeological experience on legitimate projects. More than 80 men systematically developed a set of trails within the site and settled down to exploit it, much as miners would map out and dig a mother lode."

It has been estimated that millions of dollars in Maya antiquities from Río Azul have been flown out from the nearby airfield at Dos Lagunas and sold to collectors. Most of these artifacts will never be placed under a scholar's lamp. There are new tools and techniques, however, to aid scientists in sleuthing. Interpretations of artistic styles have been narrowed. The secrets of many hieroglyphs have been revealed, and now there is something called "neutron activation analysis" that can be used actually to determine the source of pottery vessels.

Partly because of the enormous flood of Maya antiquities that poured into the United States from Río Azul, U.S. Secretary of State George Schultz and Foreign Minister Fernando Andrade of Guatemala signed a treaty in 1984. The document banned importation into the United States of any antique ceramics from the Peten region.

A UNESCO treaty banning the import of national treasures from Third World countries has never been ratified by most European countries, including Britain, Switzerland, and France. These countries say they will never ratify such a treaty.

NAKUM (PLACE OF BOWLS)

Northwest of El Naranjo and situated on the gently sloping banks of the Río Holmul are the ruins of Nakum. Certainly not the place of bowls any longer. The site is, literally, ringed with the campsites of looters. To be accurate, some of these campsites may have been those of chicleros, but judging by the broken potsherds we found in many camps, most of them had served güecheros.

Nakum is a Classic site, constructed during a period of Maya expansion, A.D. 731 to 790. In 1910 Alfred M. Tozzer, from Harvard's Peabody Museum, wrote, "Tikal is the most important of sites in the Peten district. Nakum undoubtedly comes in second in point of size and from the point of view of architectural remains." Tozzer went on to comment on the paucity of design at Nakum, calling it "severity carried to the extreme."

Early explorers discovered a palace there that contained forty-four rooms, a size unique throughout the land of the Maya. This grand building has long since succumbed to time and fallen in.

In a comparison of buildings at Nakum and other sites, it has been postulated that as many as fifty thousand people lived at or around Nakum.

YAXHA (GREEN WATER)

During Late Classic times, which were tumultuous for the Lowland Maya, many people concentrated around Lakes Peten, Macanche, and Yaxha (the second largest lake in El Peten) and built centers. The site of Yaxha, occupied from the first through the tenth centuries, was such a city.

Over five hundred structures have been mapped at Yaxha; when comparisons were made with the nearby city of Tikal, it was found that the density of structures at Yaxha was over a third greater than at Tikal. Yaxha was the only other site to have erected a twin pyramid complex—marking a *katun* (twenty-year period) ending—like those at Tikal. Estimates of population at Yaxha have gone as high as fifty thousand.

An early explorer, Teobert Maler, published a report in 1904. He wrote:

It is easy to imagine how the architectural arrangement of the city—a long line of monumental structures surrounded by thousands of cabins—must have offered great convenience to the people at large. The inhabitants had but a few steps to take down the gentle slope of the declivity on the south to reach the clear waters of the lake, while toward the north stretched boundless plains inviting the cultivation of maize. No doubt thousands of cayucos or dugouts, cruised in all directions on the waters of the lake in those distant days.

Maler also remarked that the water had risen considerably in the 1800s.

He added, "I should like to direct the attention of future travelers to the further observation of this phenomenon, which has not reached a climax."

The rainy seasons of 1979 and 1980 were much heavier than usual. A serious situation was no doubt abetted by the thousands of new settlers who flocked into Peten in the early 1970s when the roads were built and land was offered. Knowing no better, these settlers cut down and burned thousands of acres, thus destroying much of the watershed. As a result, the waters in the lakes of El Peten rose dramatically. By the late eighties, the causeway leading into Yaxha lay several feet beneath the surface of the lake.

There were only three carved stelae discovered at Yaxha. Two of them were badly eroded and considered worthless by looters. The third is in relatively good shape and has been well guarded since its discovery. The site is pockmarked with tunnels and pits, some as a result of legitimate excavations, others not.

TOPOXTE (BUSH BEARING HOLLOW SEEDS)

At the west end of Lake Yaxche lie several small islands, and on three of them are the ruins of Topoxte (named by Teobert Maler). The site was occupied from Preclassic through terminal Postclassic times. It was evidently another site that attracted people during troubled times. Topoxte remained alive and well several centuries after the fall of mighty Tikal, despite their being less than twenty miles apart. Looters have had their way with Topoxte. Time has also been very unkind to this small site. There is a photographic record of Topoxte's crumbling. Harvard archaeologist James Bullard wrote:

Although previously described only cursorily, Structure C at Topoxté probably has been known to archaeologists longer than any other ancient building in the department of El Petén. From existing records, it is possible to follow the building's deterioration as it gradually gives way before the destructive elements of the tropical forest growth. The litter of censers (incense burners) on the floor shows that the roof must have fallen soon after abandonment— perhaps at the time of abandonment. In 1831 the lintel beams were still in place over the doorways. Comparisons of Maler's 1904 photograph with Lundell's of 1933 reveals that, during the interval, the southeast corner of the superstructure had collapsed, and the upper part of the south stairwell of the main stairway had eroded back. Between 1933 and 1958, when I first photographed structure C, there appears to have been a collapse of the northeast corner of the super-structure as well as considerable damage to the lowest sub-structure terrace on the south side. When I last visited Topoxté in 1960, additional sections of structure C were in danger of falling.

By 1979, all that remained of Structure C were a mound of rubble and a partial stairwell.

Ixlu

Ixlu is another small Late Classic site that people evidently flocked to after the collapse of many larger centers such as Tikal. The date on a stela found there reads A.D. 879, a time several years after the abandonment of Tikal.

Some barely discernable stonework can be seen at the top of one temple, and pottery sherds are scattered about. Once considered little more than rubble, the leavings of looters (broken pottery, bone splinters, looted tombs, and so forth) are presently receiving more attention than in the past. Many scientists think that if nothing is done to protect small, remote sites, rubble may be all that is left for future scholars to study.

Tikal (Place Where Spirit Voices Are Heard)

Tikal, the grandest of all the ancient Maya cities found in Guatemala, has been the object of more scholarly prying, more restoration, more theories, more calculations, and more sweat-sodden work than any other Maya center in Mesoamerica.

After being rediscovered in 1848, Tikal lay untouched until the University of Pennsylvania began an ambitious program of study and restoration in 1956 that ended in 1978. (Restoration and study is currently carried on by the Guatemalans.) Research teams found that the site had first been occupied around 600 B.C. Three hundred years later, descendants of these early pioneers began to build a civilization that would endure for another thousand years.

Scientists decided that the site had originally been selected because it rose, on several small hills, some two hundred feet above the huge surrounding seasonal *bajos* (swamps). This was a fact that did not surprise Edwin Shook, the first field director of the Pennsylvania project. He told me once that he did not think the Maya liked "getting their feet wet any more than we did." Abundant deposits of chert and flint helped Tikal become a major supplier of tools and weapons and an important trade center.

The ease with which the site is reached and certain amenities available there are, no doubt, at least partially responsible for Tikal's popularity in recent years. A grass airstrip (later covered with asphalt) was hewn out of the jungle. This was followed shortly by a hotel of sorts, aptly named The Jungle Lodge. Tourists by the dozens, then the hundreds, and finally by the thousands began pouring into the site. In the beginning they came on ancient DC-3s and DC-6s, soon replaced by Convairs and air buses. One afternoon, I saw fourteen planes lined up on the small tarmac at the end of the runway. Flights became so numerous that authorities were forced to shut down the airstrip permanently in the early 1980s. It seems that vibrations from motors on the low-flying planes had begun to cause damage to some of the structures.

The amount of work carried on at Tikal so far is prodigious, the amount remaining even more so. William Coe, also a project director, stated: "Perhaps as many as 10,000 earlier platforms and buildings lie sealed beneath the surface features mapped during 1957 to 1960. Excavations here revealed at least 1,100 years of apparently ceaseless construction. Stone monuments were erected at the site for 900 to 1,000 years. Over 1,000,000 tools, ceremonial objects, personal ornaments and other items have been unearthed during the work of the Tikal project." Remember, these figures were for nearly three decades past! Coe went on to say that he believes it will take a century or so to thoroughly investigate buried buildings in central Tikal alone.

In one sense, Tikal has been spared. Looting occurs there, but certainly on a minor scale in comparison with that in other sites. There are simply too many people around at all times for anything major to be carried out. On the other hand, Tikal might be held responsible for the tremendous interest in—and owning of—artifacts that really began in the sixties. When it became apparent that people would pay a great deal of money for old Maya things, a new and destructive industry was spawned.

UAXACTUN (EIGHT STONE)

About twelve miles north of the great Maya center of Tikal lie the ruins of Uaxactun. This site came under intense study by the Carnegie Institute from 1926 through 1937. Studies of ceramics turned up there laid the foundation for the whole of Lowland Maya chronology.

Uaxactun is one of the oldest Lowland Maya sites. The earliest date mentioned on inscriptions there is A.D. 328. The Maya at Uaxactun were constructing new buildings as late as A.D. 850, with the last dynastic monument dated A.D. 889, ten years later than Tikal's final inscription.

As at Tikal, scientists determined that people lived at Uaxactun long after the site ceased to function as a city or center. Uaxactun also has the distinction of being the first Classic site with an astronomical observatory.

Excitement over the discovery of two Maya books found in tombs quickly turned to disappointment when it was discovered that the pages of the books had been cemented together by the centuries of hot, humid weather. Maya books were folded like an accordion. Fibers from the copa tree were pounded into sheets, then covered with limestone plaster on which the scribes wrote. Only three such Maya books have survived to the present.

As in almost every site, there are the trademarks left by looters. Pits and tunnels intrude into mounds. Artifacts, mainly in the forms of vases and bowls, have surfaced in collections throughout the world. There have been guardianes at the site for several years, stopping the most blatant looting, but tourists visiting the site can often buy something from people of the small village whose huts are lined up along the grass strip runway.

The Maya themselves must have at least shared in the destruction of their own art. In Uaxactun as well as Tikal, the most recent of the great palaces and temples were built upon the ruins of their predecessors. Stelae, bowls, carvings, and other works of art were ruthlessly destroyed and used as rubble to fill in new constructions.

There exists a not-very-credible Indian story about of how the site got its name. When local Indians asked the first archaeologists where they came from, they were told, Washington. The Indians turned this into Wah-shock-TOON.

EL BEJUCAL (THE PLACE OF WATER VINES)

A small site close to Uaxactun, El Bejucal has been known of for a long time. The site takes its name from an abundance of *bejuco* in the area. Of the myriad *lianas* (vines) used by the people living and working in El Peten, the *bejuco de agua* is of singular importance. It is a large vine often growing several inches thick, and when a section is cut at an angle the vine yields a clear, sweet water. In an area abundant with the vine, workers, mostly chicleros and *shateros,* are able to fill a fifty-gallon drum with water from this plant in a very short time. Shateros are men who make a living wandering through the jungle collecting a plant known as *shati.* This plant has the ability to stay green and fresh looking for long periods. It is highly prized by florists in the United States for making wreaths. At Christmas and Easter time, daily flights of airplanes crammed with cargoes of shati leave Flores destined for Miami and flower shops throughout the United States.

At the site, a single large, plain, badly eroded stela stands in front of a debris-covered mound. It became apparent to us on a visit that El Bejucal once had a number of carved stelae. Shattered stelae fragments, some bearing carvings, were spread about. Even these fragments were gone when we visited the site again a few months later.

EL ZOTZ (THE PLACE OF BATS)

El Zotz, a very large Maya site just north of Lake Peten Itza, will surely prove to be very important. It is a relatively new find of the seventies. Despite the site's close proximity to a main road, it long went unreported.

To anyone walking through this extensive ancient city, damage by looters is apparent at every hand. Stelae are shattered, with the best carvings hauled away. Tunnels are everywhere. Guardianes now at the site told us that eighty-four illegal tunnels were found there. The loss of priceless artifacts and knowledge can only be imagined.

No carved stela has been found intact as yet. Remains of elaborate stucco works can be seen. Looters, in their efforts to find a tomb in one temple, partially uncovered a large, beautifully crafted stucco figure. The figure still had visible traces of paint when it was first uncovered. Exposure to the elements has since worn any paint away.

At one end of Zotz, about an hour's walk from the main plaza, wending its way through a number of structures, the gradually ascending trail brings one to El Templo del Diablo (The Temple of the Devil). There is no sinister implication in the name, which was bestowed upon the temple in honor of the man nicknamed "Diablo" who discovered it. At the top of this temple viewers are presented with a stunning view of El Peten. A seemingly endless jungle stretches away several hundred feet below. Across this bright green ocean of trees, standing out like a great white sail on the far eastern horizon, stands the roof comb of Temple IV at Tikal.

At dusk each day, bats pour forth in uncountable numbers from nearby cliffs. It is from them that El Zotz takes its modern name.

MOTUL DE SAN JOSÉ

The shores and surrounding areas of Lake Peten Itza are dotted with the remains of Maya sites. An hour's walk north of the huge lake brings the traveler to the ruins of Motul de San José. In 1895 Teobert Maler photographed a stela that featured two figures carved in a dancing attitude. Looking at his marvelous photograph, one can see that the monument was extremely rich in detail, flawlessly executed. The stela is all but destroyed now; only about a third remains.

Our Indian guide explained what had happened. According to this man, sometime in the not-too-distant past an old campesino (farmer) chopped down the surrounding forest to prepare his milpa. After the cut-down bush and trees had dried in the searing summer sun, and on a propitious day no doubt portended by a shaman, the old fellow fired the field. Tempera-

tures reached during the burning of a milpa are tremendous. The fire was too much for this monument, and it literally exploded.

Before sophistication set in—that is to say, before stone saws and other modern equipment, including helicopters, became available to looters—one of the methods used to reduce stelae (which often weighed several tons) to more manageable weights was to build a fire around the monument, keeping it going for hours. When it was judged ready, the very hot stone was doused with water and would instantly fragment. When they were cool, pieces were hauled away. There were obvious drawbacks—monuments so treated would frequently explode so thoroughly that little was left.

TAYASAL, OR FLORES

Founded by immigrants from Chichen Itza around A.D. 1194, Tayasal (now known as Flores) endured until the year 1697 before becoming the final victim of the Spanish conquest. Nearly all of the Maya had been subjugated over a hundred years before Tayasal fell.

The Spaniards knew of the island stronghold in Lake Peten Itza. Pedro Alvarado had visited Tayasal in 1524 on his epic march through El Peten, on his way to punish errant Spaniards in Honduras.

In 1696 a Spanish priest traveled to Tayasal in an attempt to bring the Itza people into the Catholic church. This priest knew and understood the Maya calendar. He realized that a period of great change was portended by Maya prophecy, and he used this argument in an attempt to bring the last of the Maya into Christendom. The ruler of the Maya recognized the logic in the priest's entreaties, but asked that he and his people be granted a four-month waiting period. It was not to be. A Spanish army, led by Martín de Ursua, arrived on the shores of Lake Peten Itza and began building a large galley. When the boat was finished, the Spanish began their war against the Itza. It was soon over, the slaughter said to be terrible. A terrified populace fled the island, many of them drowning in their attempt to escape. Not a single Spanish soldier was lost in the battle. Historians wonder if perhaps the prophecy of great change did not play a large part in the lack of resistance at the fall of Tayasal.

After the island was taken, so great was the number of effigies and idols remaining that, according to the record, it took the entire Spanish army from nine in the morning until half past five in the afternoon to destroy them. The destruction included several Maya books. The very few remaining books that were discovered there centuries later by archaeologists had their pages so stuck together that they proved useless.

There is a recorded version of how one Maya god came to be. When Pedro Alvarado passed by Tayasal in 1524, he had left a lame horse in the care of the Maya. He failed, however, to leave adequate feeding instructions. The Maya fed the animal only flowers and turkey stew. Perhaps it was the diet, or perhaps it was the wound the horse suffered; at any rate, the animal died. The Maya, fearing what might happen to them upon the return of the Spanish, carved a horse from stone and set it up.

As time passed, the cult of the stone horse grew in importance, until finally it was worshiped as Tzimin Chac, or Thunder Horse. (The Maya believed that the noise from firearms actually came from the Spanish horses.) In 1618 a visiting priest became so incensed at this blasphemy that he picked up a rock and destroyed the idol. The Maya, still fearing what would happen when the returning Spanish found their horse destroyed, tried to transport the stone pieces over to the mainland and hide them. The story goes, however, that the overloaded dugout canoe carrying the pieces overturned in the middle of Lake Peten Itza, and the stone horse was lost forever.

EL PERU

Far to the north in El Peten, close to the border shared with Mexico, lies what is left of El Peru. It is a wasteland of broken stelae, shattered altars, pits, and tunnels. Evidence indicates that this is another Maya site that was at the mercy of looters for a long time. Thieves may have been interrupted at their work; after several monuments were broken up into manageable pieces, many were left, carelessly strewn about. It was as if a huge bomb had been dropped at El Peru, blasting everything apart!

Armed guards have been stationed at the site for several years, and looting has stopped.

LA FLORIDA (THE PLACE OF FLOWERS), OR OCULTUN

Archaeologist and explorer Edwin M. Shook came across the ruins of Ocultun while he was engaged on a rubber-tree hunting expedition for the United States during the Second World War. Located on the bank of the Río San Pedro in northern El Peten, what is now known as La Florida was occupied from Preclassic to Late Classic times. It consists of a complex of temples and other structures raised on pyramids, with small plazas and courtyards.

Progress was the main culprit causing destruction at Ocultun. The government-owned airline, Aviateca, bull-dozed an airstrip straight through the ruins for its weekly flights. It is oil country now, and there is a lot of construction going on, including new roads.

On our visit in the late seventies, the standing masonry described by Shook was no longer apparent. What remained were a few small, brush-covered mounds and one fallen stela in situ. Another monument, badly eroded, has been moved to the backyard of a local official.

The local people, as well as several maps, refer to this location as El Naranjo, but it is not to be confused with the Maya site of El Naranjo that is several hundred kilometers to the east.

PIEDRAS NEGRAS (BLACK STONES)

Working in the upper reaches of the Usumacinta River in 1895, early German explorer Teobert Maler learned from Indians of the existence of several so-called "lost cities." He determined that Piedras Negras was the largest and set out to locate it. Maler found Piedras Negras on the east bank of the Usumacinta, near the Mexican border in northwestern El Peten. It was, of necessity, constructed on steep hills somewhat back from the river. (The Usumacinta fluctuates wildly between the dry and wet season.)

At the time of Maler's discovery, buildings at Piedras Negras were in a bad state, the jungle having had its way for centuries. Despite evidence of depredations, much of it carried out by Mexicans crossing the nearby border, there were several nearly intact, well-carved stelae. The Maya practice at Piedras Negras had been to erect a monument at each *hotun* (five-year period) ending. Interestingly, Quirigua, many miles to the southeast, was the only other Maya city to consistently erect monuments commemorating ho-tuns. Of the twenty-two stelae at Piedras Negras, all are accounted for. The earliest date carved there is A.D. 534, the latest, A.D. 810.

A great archaeological breakthrough came as a result of a prodigious amount of work at Piedras Negras carried out by Tatiana Proskouriakoff in the sixties. She put to rest the heretofore held theory that the figures carved on the great stone monuments were gods. Rather, she proved that they were mortal men and women—rulers, priests, lords, and other important dignitaries. She further proved that accompanying hieroglyphic texts recorded important events in their lives such as births, deaths, ascendancies to power, military triumphs, and, sometimes, records of progeny. Her proofs, which shattered many pet notions, are still having an effect on Mayanists.

SAN DIEGO

The influx of people in a colonization program intended to populate El Peten, coupled with attending roads cut through the jungle (in particular, to the new oil-field discoveries in the north), have caused many new, often small, sites to come to light. San Diego was reported to the authorities in 1980. The site lies just a few meters off a jungle road leading to northwest Guatemala. San Diego is a Late Classic site, and takes its name from Laguna San Diego, which lies a few miles away.

Ancient Maya artisans carved a two-meter figure on the face of a limestone cliff at the site, forty feet up from the base. It may be that the Maya of San Diego used a shortcut, carving the figure on the cliff rather than building a temple. Getting a good view of the figure is difficult. The carving would best be seen from the bottom of the hill that the cliff tops, but at present the surrounding jungle prevents this.

The photographing of this unique artifact proved strenuous. Support platforms for the heavy generator, along with a very tall ladder, had to be built of materials found at hand. Watching

Peteneros demonstrate their ability to overcome obstacles such as heights and weights, using only poles, vines, and other natural products of the woods and very often having no more than a machete for a tool, one is struck by their ingenuity. Not unlike their illustrious ancestors, the modern Maya can accomplish astounding results with seemingly few resources.

POLOL (WATER HOLE)

Just inside the rain forest on the edge of the vast grasslands called savannahs, about seven kilometers from La Libertad, are the ruins of Polol. A joint botanical expedition from the University of Michigan and Carnegie Institute in 1933 happened upon the ruins. Except for cursory mapping and exploration, little archaeological investigation has been carried out at Polol.

A huge pyramid—with base measurements of three hundred and twenty-five by three hundred and ninety feet—dominates the entire site. This great structure reaches a height of one hundred and sixty-five feet and supports ruined temple chambers at the top. The Maya cleverly incorporated the natural formation of a limestone knoll into the base of the pyramid. Dates deciphered from stelae place Polol in the Late Classic era.

A report from 1933 reads: "The locality, bush and savannah where the ruins are located is called Polol. This is the name for an *aguada* (water hole) near the site. Polol is an aquatic sedge that was formerly found at the water hole."

Polol has been well excavated, but not by the right people. The floors of the chambers on top of the great pyramid have been destroyed; the entire area is pockmarked with exploratory pits. As evidenced by potsherds strewn about some of these pits, looters have had some success.

ITSIMTE (SMALL YELLOW PLANT)

A small yellow-flowered plant that tastes and smells like anise, called *itsimte* by the Indians and found at the site in abundance, gave Itsimte its name. The plant, often brewed into a flavorsome tea, is presently called *pericón* after a small yellow-headed parrot known as a *perico*. Itsimte is also used to flavor posole, a drink made from ground maize and water.

The ruins are situated about fifteen kilometers north of the town of La Libertad in the vast savannahs of El Peten. The town was formerly called Sacluk, a Maya name. There is not much beyond a few grass-and-bush-covered mounds at Itsimte today. All of the mounds have been disturbed by looters.

Teobert Maler, not overly politic in expressing his opinions, had this to say on the subject of changing the name of Sacluk to La Libertad:

The present ruling class (1905), which has not the slightest interest in historical names, will not permit this modest place to continue under its Maya name, and has changed it to "Libertad." Many of the ancient American names of places have been forgotten because the Spanish replaced most of them by names of Christian Saints, and owing to the present mischievous custom of supplanting them by political catchwords, such as Progreso, Reforma, and Libertad, or names of dubious champions of liberty. Of course it does not improve the condition of affairs because the people continue to find it easier to alter names rather that to make roads and build bridges.

I think that the men who work in the jungles of El Peten have refined this custom into a subtle joke. On more than one occasion we would come across a camp used by chicleros, shateros, or güecheros, abandoned now except for armies of ravenous fleas and ticks. The area was almost always littered with empty, rusted cans, tattered pieces of plastic nylon, and general filth. When I turned to my Indian companion and asked disgustedly, "What *is* this place?" he would almost always come up with a tongue-in-cheek answer such as El Paradiso (Paradise), Buena Fey (Good Faith), or El Divino (The Divine Place).

ITZAN

In 1968 a survey team determining the boundaries for a new settlement (part of a government-sponsored colonization program for El Peten) came across the remains of an ancient city. It was named Itzan.

Itzan is located on a high bluff overlooking a lagoon and the Arroyo Itzan (from which it takes its name) that flows into the Río Pasión. Potsherds collected there by members of the Harvard Peabody Museum expedition (then working far upriver at Seibal) proved to be mainly from the Late Classic era, with a few that were Preclassic in origin.

A fair-sized town, now covering the site of Itzan, sprang up before more than cursory scientific examinations could take place. Needless to say, locals have thoroughly examined the site on their own. A night spent there almost always brought a soft cough at the door of our tent, with a local offering some artifact that he had found (never dug up!) while he was preparing his milpa.

La Amelia

La Amelia, El Caribe, and Aguas Calientes are three small ruins located close to the Río Pasión, west of the present-day town of Sayaxche.

Famous early explorer and archaeologist Sylvanus Morley wrote of these sites: "This combined group, according to the scanty evidence available, seems to have been in a position to erect sculptured stone monuments probably of the lahuntun (ten year period) and katun (twenty year period) endings only."

Morley predicted that a monument dated A.D. 800 would turn up one day. Over half a century later, Ian Graham found a stela in fragments at the ruins of La Amelia. His workers transported the pieces to the nearby town of Sayaxche, where it was reassembled. Everything about the stela, including the date, fit Morley's prediction.

Dos Pilas (Two Stelae), formerly Dos Posas (Two Springs)

This Late Classic site was the ruling center for the Patixbatun basin of El Peten. There are several sites close by, including Aguateca, Tamarindita, Arroyo de Piedra, and La Amelia.

The jungle kept the secret of Dos Pilas until 1960. We first visited the site a few years later; it became a favorite place for us. We lived on the Laguna Patixbatun for several years and visited Dos Pilas at every opportunity.

In 1989 Vanderbilt University began a program of investigation and reconstruction with plans for several years of study. Before research began, the university built an extensive center at Dos Pilas complete with a dining hall, a medical clinic with a full-time resident doctor, and modern labs with computers and other sophisticated equipment.

The team of scholars has concluded that the entire area—extending for nearly a hundred miles in some directions—was concerned with little else but war and conquest. Dos Pilas is one of the few Lowland Maya centers that constructed defensive walls. Many of the stelae, there as well as at other sites close by, show ruler/warriors holding spears and protective shields. Carved steps show bound prisoners.

In the early sixties, just before the worldwide market for *anything* pre-Columbian exploded, small artifacts often lay unmolested for centuries. In the early seventies, looters armed with stonecutting saws cut up and hauled away one of the best-preserved stelae at Dos Pilas. The government acted quickly in placing several armed guardianes at the site, and effectively shut down any more serious looting attempts.

It is now thought that an offshoot of Tikal's royal lineage may have founded Dos Pilas. The emblem glyphs for both sites are similar.

What was probably a satellite of Dos Pilas was discovered in 1975, just a ten-minute walk from the center of Dos Pilas. It is called Los Duendes (The Dwarfs) because of the depiction of dwarfs carved on stelae there.

Arroyo de Piedra (River of Stone)

Another small site, about an hour and a half's walk from Dos Pilas, was also discovered in 1975. Stela 1 at Arroyo de Piedra bears a date of May 12, A.D. 613, the earliest date found on any stela in the Patixbatun basin.

Stela 2 at the site is badly fragmented, but would have stood over thirteen feet tall when erected. The head of this figure alone measures three by three and one-half feet. Tikal's emblem glyph is included in the hieroglyphic text carved on this monument.

Tamarindito (Little Tamarind)

The fruit of the tamarind tree, which consists of large seeds covered by tangy pulp, is used to make a refreshing drink.

While looking for oil, Esso Company personnel came across Tamarindito in 1959. Thought to be a small Late Classic site, it once featured a carved stairway depicting several bound prisoners. This motif is common at sites in the Patixbatun basin. On nearly all bound-prisoner stairways, the figure is shown in the same position, reclining on its right side, with the left leg raised and thrown over the right, looking over a shoulder in the same direction.

These stair panels at Tamarindito appear to have been easy booty. I know of one entire panel that graces the side of a home in Antigua, hundreds of kilometers away. I mention this to point out the fact that very few people seem to care what happens to these National treasures, except, of course, for their monetary value. A few dedicated people fight to save them, but the rest do not really concern themselves until something comes up missing, and then everyone becomes highly indignant!

Aguateca

Defense was of prime concern for the Maya when they constructed this small Late Classic center. It is said to be a copy of nearby Dos Pilas. Situated on a high bluff overlooking the Laguna Patixbatun, Aguateca is enclosed by a roughly horseshoe-shaped deep chasm. The chasm is breached by six stone bridges, four of which the inhabitants blockaded with stone walls. Carved dates on stelae at Aguateca span just over one hundred years.

Aguateca lay mostly unmolested through time, ignored by all but a few archaeologists and knowledgeable tourists. In 1976, however, Stela 3, which had been supported in an erect position by the trunk of an *indio desnudo* (naked Indian) tree, along with a portion of another stela, was missing from the site.

Cancuen (Nest of Snakes)

Eighty-one miles upriver from the village of Sayaxche on the Río Pasión are the ruins of ancient Cancuen. These rest on a high bluff overlooking the river. The Pasión fluctuates several meters from the wet season to the dry, which probably played a part in Cancuen's location. Occupation of Cancuen continued past A.D. 830, making it one of the last Maya sites in El Peten. It was also the largest site on the Río Pasión. It has been pointed out that the longevity and size of Cancuen are perhaps due to the fact that the site was a sort of way station between the Lowland and Highland Maya.

There is nothing left at the site that can be called visually impressive Maya architecture. What is left are low, brush-covered mounds, riddled with the usual exploratory pits.

A unique type of stela, stepped at the top, with large holes worked completely through the monument, originated at Cancuen. A very early and famous archaeologist, Alfred Maudsley, gave this imaginative description: "It may be assumed that the victims were bound by means of the perforations to these stelae, the sacrifice probably being usually performed with the victim in an upright position before stelae of this kind."

Sheer ignorance and total lack of thought have often been responsible for the destruction of Maya artifacts. On his journey to Cancuen, Maudsley stopped to investigate the report of two standing stelae at a small site known locally as La Reforma. He wrote later:

Just before leaving this monteria (a small jungle encampment) its wretched encargado, Prisciliano Colorado, conceived the idea of building an oven, for the purpose of baking bread in order to use up an insignificant remnant of flour, a most unnecessary proceeding, considering the limited amount of flour left on his hands. Although there were plenty of other stones to be found, these two stelae were selected and broken into little pieces to build his miserable oven, which was no sooner finished and, probably, but once used, than, as needs must be in the nature of the case, it was immediately abandoned. Instead, therefore, of examining and photographing bas-reliefs, we only had the pleasure of beholding the oven of Prisciliano Colorado. If you take into account the pricelessness of the raw material used in its construction, this was undoubtedly the most expensive oven ever built.

Tres Islas (Three Islands)

Tres Islas is a small Early Classic Maya site thirteen kilometers inland from the Río Pasión and directly north of Cancuen.

Maya sites were often located at roughly equal distances from one another. Tres Islas is equidistant from Cancuen and Machaquila. The placement of Tikal, Zotz, and Yaxha is another example. Many Mayanists think that this placement was deliberate and that something close to our state and county system may have been employed.

Only debris-covered mounds await future archaeologists at Tres Islas.

MACHAQUILA

In spite of being just over twenty-five miles to the southeast of Sayaxche, Machaquila stands out as perhaps the most difficult to reach site we encountered in the compilation of this book. It was also one of the saddest places we have seen.

Our walk began at Poptun and roughly followed the Machaquila River. For about half the year, swollen by the rains, the river rages with whirlpools and steep waterfalls. Huge boulders lurk beneath its roiling surface. Tame in the dry season, the river consists of interrupted stagnant pools. Navigation by canoe then is possible, but very difficult.

We walked for thirteen days, eight days in and five coming out. Our main problem concerned the mules that we took along to transport tents, cameras, food, and other supplies. A person can slip through the heavy brush that edges up to the river, but a substantial trail must be hacked out with machetes for a mule to get through.

The area is very sparsely populated; after the third day, we encountered no one.

The desolation at Machaquila affected us all when we finally arrived. There was, literally, nothing left at this once-marvelous site. Stelae left behind had become victims of stone saws

wielded by looters. Altars had been smashed; pits and tunnels covered the entire area. The few carvings that were left were too eroded to be of any use to the looters. It was obvious that several men had worked there a long time in their quest for Maya treasure.

Artifacts from Machaquila have surfaced throughout the world, mostly in private collections.

SEIBAL (PLACE OF THE CEIBA TREE)

Discovered in the late 1800s by hunters in search of the giant mahogany trees of El Peten, the site lay generally undisturbed until the University of Harvard's Peabody Museum began investigations and reconstruction in 1964.

Seibal is of particular interest to scientist and layperson alike. Few sites present such nearly pristine stelae as are found there.

Scientists are especially interested in the history of Seibal. What caused the decline that took place between the time of Christ and 650 A.D.? What triggered the burst of florescence that reached its zenith between A.D. 830 and 930? Seibal was still going strong when Tikal and Piedras Negras were well into their decline. Archaeologists believe its reversal of fortune is traceable to a foreign invasion.

Most of the figures depicted on stone monuments at Seibal are not Maya in appearance, but are dressed in Maya garb. The lords shown often have beards and moustaches and carry weapons such as atlatls (spear-throwers) and darts, weapons certainly of Mexican descent.

After the work of the Peabody Museum ended in 1968, the Guatemalan authorities immediately placed several guardianes at the site, assuring protection from looters. It has been said that Seibal proved to be a training ground for workers who, because of their acquired expertise, would later be in demand for illegal activities at other sites.

Seibal is maintained as a park and is truly one of the loveliest Maya sites.

Desecrated tombs at Naj Tunich, located on the
balcony. These structures are the first of their
kind known to have been found in a Maya cave.
The retaining wall and rooms are the only sign of
Maya architecture found at Naj Tunich.

Opposite above: This is one of the best-preserved panels of hieroglyphs at Naj Tunich. The top three rows of glyphs bear the date interpreted as December 18, A.D. 738, a time near the peak of Classic Maya culture.

Opposite below: One of the first drawings of a human figure, encountered after one travels down the Grand Concourse of Naj Tunich. This seated man, holding a decapitated head, was painted nearly twelve feet from the floor. It is the highest drawing in the cave.

Above: On the smooth wall once formed by the waters of an underground river, in a chamber at Naj Tunich that has come to be called the Bearer of Fire Room, this elegant panel of glyphs stands out in Classic style. The chamber takes its name from the fire glyph that is carried by a figure using a tumpline, or *mecapal* (second line, first glyph on the left). This beautifully rendered text yielded dates that correspond to August 25, A.D. 744, and August 20, A.D. 772. Fifteen figure drawings and five hieroglyphic texts were discovered in the Bearer of Fire Room.

Above: On market day, an Indian brings his wares to display and sell at Chichicastenango in the Guatemalan highlands. The *mecapal*, widely used today, allows men to transport large and heavy loads over a considerable distance.

Below: A seated noble, from the Bearer of Fire Room, with a face profile drawn behind him. Eighteen profiles were discovered on the walls at Naj Tunich.

A dwarf, also from the Bearer of Fire Room at Naj Tunich. *Enanos* (dwarfs) played an important part in Maya rituals, often being used as stand-ins for children chosen to be sacrificed. Dwarfs were used in the necessary rituals and pageantry until, at the last moment, the child picked for the occasion was sacrificed. Of twenty remains recovered thus far from the cave, four were those of small children and four others those of juveniles.

About five hundred meters from the entrance, along the Grand Concourse, the cave forks; the left tunnel leads to the west terminus. En route, the visitor passes through the Hall of Musicians. In this painting, known as the *musicos* (from which the cave derives its name), the figure on the left is playing a drum, while the man on the right may be holding a type of ceramic drum known to exist in Late Classic and Postclassic times. This photograph was taken just three months after the existence of Naj Tunich became public knowledge. Damage had already begun. Someone had touched and smeared the throat of the left-hand figure.

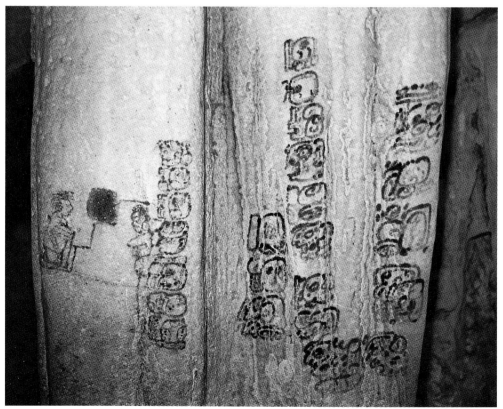

Opposite above: Musical instruments, particularly the drum and flute, still play a very important part in the lives of the Maya. Here, two drums and a flute are used by modern Maya Indians to summon believers to a mass at the cathedral in Antigua.

Opposite below: Further along the west tunnel of Naj Tunich is the Chamber of Crystal Columns, with its ballplayer scene and panel of glyphs drawn by an ancient scribe on a calcite column. Just after its discovery, an attempt was made to remove this panel by cutting the column off with a chain saw.

Above: Here in the Hall of Balam, named for the glyph David Stuart interpreted as Jaguar, is the largest panel of glyphs found at Naj Tunich.

These four photos are close-up views of the Jaguar panel of glyphs in the Hall of Balam at Naj Tunich. In the top left photo the Jaguar glyph is in the second row, third glyph from the top.

Above: Near the terminus of the right-hand tunnel at Naj Tunich, apart from the other paintings, one finds the two seated figures shown here. They have been tentatively identified by Michael Coe as the Hero Twins, Hunahpu and Xbalanque, from the *Popul Vuh,* the Maya book of the dawn of life and sacred book of the Quiche Maya.

Below: Gracefully seated on a small throne, this Naj Tunich figure gestures toward a bowl that appears to hold something smoking, possibly an offering of copal (pom).

Opposite: Pom is still the favorite offering used by the Maya today, who believe prayers are carried to the gods in the smoke.

From the section of Naj Tunich's left tunnel known as the Passage of Rites, twenty figures and twelve texts were discovered. This painting has sparked a great deal of controversy. Some call it the rape scene; others see testicles on the right-hand figure, suggesting homosexual content. Still others are convinced that the right-hand figure is that of an archetypal female, or the moon goddess. The moon goddess is the patroness of the month called Ch'en by the Yucatec Maya. Ch'en refers to a hole in the ground such as a cave or *cenote* (underground well).

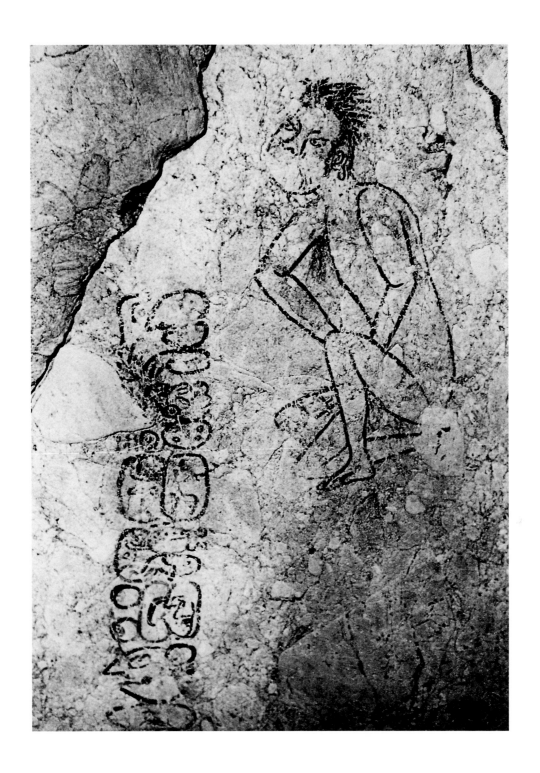

This extraordinary drawing and accompanying glyphic text are also from the Passage of Rites at Naj Tunich. The figure is shown in a rare three-quarter view. He is holding his scarified penis, probably drawing blood for a sacred offering.

The lower figure, in a chest girdle, kneepad, and jaguar skin, stands in front of a stepped ball court with the ball and the Maya figure nine on top. The Naj Tunich depiction may be that of Hunahpu, one of the Hero Twins of the *Popul Vuh*. The scantily bearded figure at the top, with a queen conch shell in front of him, sits in calm serenity.

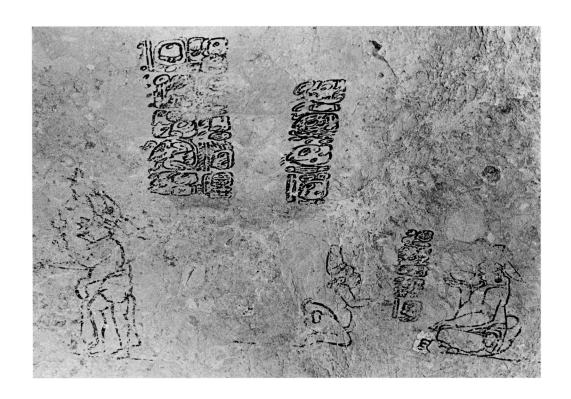

Above: Another panel of figures and texts from the Passage of Rites at Naj Tunich. The figure at the left is a dancer, wearing a deer headdress and shaking a rattle. On the right, a complacent, well-fed lord, also wearing some sort of deer head-dress, holds a bowl in his hand. The posture of the dwarf sitting across from the lord strongly suggests that he would like to be helpful.

Below: A small, gracefully drawn Naj Tunich figure gazes upward, perhaps performing an act of self-sacrifice.

In the western tunnel, painted on a sharply edged limestone column, is the longest vertical, two-column text of hieroglyphs in the cave. It disclosed a date of May 25, A.D. 771, making the text one of the last to be recorded at Naj Tunich.

Just around the sharp edge of the column at Naj Tunich, another vertical text begins with a date of May 11, A.D. 755.

Above: Standing by itself, this panel is the longest horizontal hieroglyphic text at Naj Tunich.

Below: Another figure from the Passage of Rites at Naj Tunich, also probably drawing blood for an offering.

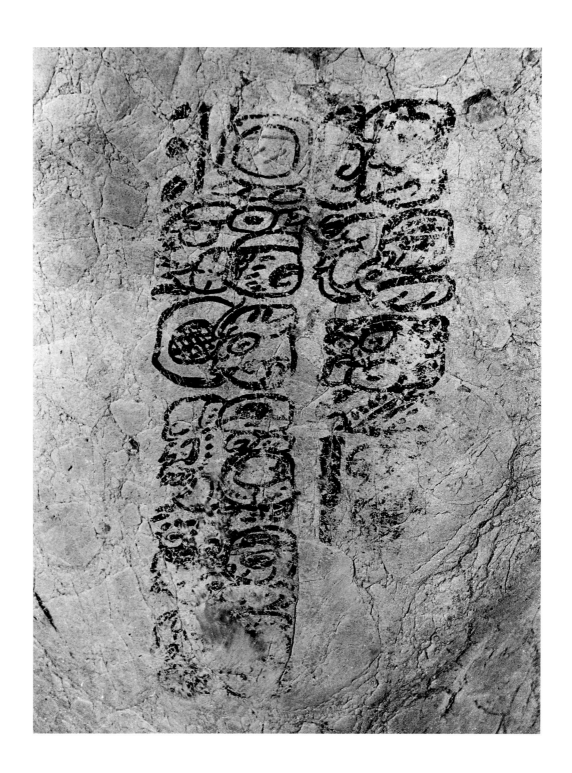

Above and opposite: Two examples of ten texts from Naj Tunich, which contain dates archaeologists determined impossible (too far apart to match the remainder of the text).

92

Opposite and below: Three of the eighteen human profiles found on the walls of Naj Tunich. **Above:** Standing figure at Naj Tunich, with a profile of the sun god in front.

Above: Slender-waisted and wide-hipped standing Naj Tunich figure with a companion seated in
front.
Below: A small kneeling figure at Naj Tunich.

Above: Hieroglyphic text from the fallen stela at Sacul (pictured in the photo below).

Below: Toppled sometime in the past, this broken stela at Sacul awaits reerection or perhaps transportation to the national museum in Guatemala City—that is, if it can escape the stone saws of the looters. A newly discovered site need only be left alone for a very short time before the well-organized thieves loot it.

Above: This small carved altar is from the site of El Naranjo.

Below: From the site of Ucanal, Stela 4 bears a late date of A.D. 849. Notice the floating figure at the top of the monument.

Opposite: Stela 20 from El Naranjo now stands in the government agency FYDYP yard in Santa Elena, El Peten. Its hieroglyphs date it A.D. 714. The figure stands on a bound prisoner.

Stela 38 from El Naranjo, assigned a date of A.D. 593, is also on display in the FYDYP yard. Its hieroglyphs are crudely done, barely scratched in the stone. Often the faces on stelae have been destroyed. It was a practice of the Maya to do so; some authorities say it was done symbolically to kill the spirit of the stone.

Monument 25 was discovered where it had fallen and shattered at El Naranjo. The pieces were laboriously transported to the border town of Melchor de Mencos, where it was reassembled and now graces the front of the town's municipal building.

When El Naranjo's Stela 10 was discovered by early archaeologist Teobert Maler, he reported that deep pits on the stone were natural and that the Maya had filled them in with plaster. The two columns of hieroglyphs bear the dedicatory date of A.D. 810, making Stela 10 a late monument.

Facing the central panel in the tomb of Ruler X at Río Azul, which holds the date, we see the figure painted on the left.

Above left: As we face the date panel at Río Azul, this depiction of Kinich Ahau, the Maya sun god, is to the right of the central panel.

Above right: A niche had been built into each side of the tomb of Ruler X at Río Azul. The niches probably once held vases or bowls containing food for the dead noble's journey through the underworld.

Opposite: This wall panel and a mat symbol were duplicated on each side at the back of the Río Azul tomb. Archaeologists believe the mat is a symbol of authority.

101

Above: From the solstice-equinox plaza of the ancient Maya city of Nakum, close to the Río Homul, Temple A thrusts its roof comb above the surrounding jungle. The two outer doorways of the chambers at the top were plastered by Maya architects so that they resemble true arches. A closer look revealed that they are corbeled arches, for which the Maya are famous.

Below: The forests of El Peten are home to thousands of strange creatures, one of which is known as the peanut-headed fulgorid. As for most living things, the Maya have a myth about this insect. I was told that if a man were bitten by the peanut head, he must have sexual intercourse with—and this was stressed—a *beautiful* woman. When I pointed out to my Indian friends that the fulgorid had no mandibles to bite with but rather fed through a sucking tube, my explanation did not get far. One Indian remarked that if he even *thought* he had been bitten, he "would stick to the old way!"

This drawing of a sailboat scratched in the plaster coating was discovered in one of the chambers at the top of Temple 216 at Yaxcha. Lake Yaxcha is the second largest body of water in El Peten.

Stela 11 at Yaxcha represents Tlaloc, the goggle-eyed rain god from Mexico.

Opposite: This small temple is all that remains at Topoxte, a Maya site on the small island of the same name on Lake Yaxcha. The site is also known for its small stelae and altars, none of which bore carvings but which were probably stuccoed and painted.

Above: Removed from the site known as Ixlu, Altar 1 (top) and Stela 2 (bottom) have been set upright into the wall of a basketball court on the Island of Flores. Both of these monuments have suffered wear in their contact with people over the past decade. Part of the hieroglyphic text from Altar 2 is exactly the same as text found in Dos Pilas, a site far to the southwest.

Above: Temple I, the Temple of the Giant Jaguar, has become the hallmark of Tikal. The roof comb is one hundred and forty feet from the plaza floor. It was constructed during the reign of Ah Cacau Caan Chac, around A.D. 700. A carved wooden lintel that once bridged a chamber at the top of the temple portrayed a very fat lord garbed in jaguar robes—hence the temple's name. Carved lintels from most buildings at Tikal were removed around the turn of the century and are now on display in the Basil Museum in Switzerland.

Below: Close-up of the floating figure on Stela 2 at Ixlu.

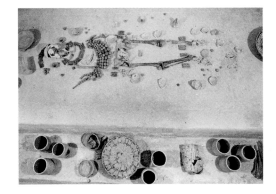

Above: Temple II, with the roof combs of Temples III (left) and IV in the background. This view is from the vaulted doorway of Temple I. There is evidence that Temple II was constructed by Ah Cacau in dedication to his wife. Known as the Temple of the Masks, it stands 120 feet high, the smallest of the five great temples at Tikal.

Below: A reconstruction of Burial 116, the tomb of Ah Cacau Caan Chac, found deep within the Temple of the Giant Jaguar. This great king, the twenty-sixth ruler of Tikal, ruled from A.D. 682 to circa 734 and was the 26th ruler of Tikal. In addition to many wonderful vases and bowls, excavators found one hundred and eighty pieces of carved jade adorning the buried figure. Burial 116 is one of the most sumptuous ever discovered.

Above: The roof comb of Temple IV, the Temple of the Double Headed Serpent (taking its name from the carved lintels), emerges from the surrounding jungle at Tikal. Constructed around A.D. 741, it towers a majestic 214 feet, remaining the tallest pre-Columbian building still standing in the Americas.

Opposite below: The North Acropolis at Tikal. In this complex alone, there are over one hundred buildings—palaces and temples—constructed one on top of another. Excavators discovered nineteen levels of consecutive construction. Earliest buildings within the complex date back to 200 B.C.

Above: The Main Plaza at Tikal, with Temple I on the left, Temple II on the right, and the un-cleared roof comb of Temple V behind the Cen-tral Acropolis. This view is from the top of the North Acropolis, pictured below.

110

Opposite above: The Nine Doorway Palace, fronting the Main Plaza and located in the Tikal group known as the Central Acropolis. The uncleared roof comb of Temple V is in the right background. Nests of *montezuma oropéndola* hang from the tree at the right.

Opposite below: A Late Classic temple emerges from beneath a thousand years of debris. Despite several decades of work at Tikal, scientists claim only a little over 1 percent of the site has been excavated.

Above: Twin Pyramid Complex Q, built to commemorate a twenty-year period, or katun. At Tikal there are six such commemorative complexes.

Opposite above: A crude carving scratched in the plaster, discovered on a wall of an excavated room in Tikal's Palace of the Channeled Grooves at Group G. This sacrificial scene is no longer visible, having fallen victim to thousands of touching tourists. The frame around the scene is the result of repairs made after thieves had tried to take it off the wall sometime in the early seventies.

Opposite below: An underground cavern or room, carved out of solid limestone. A number of these *chultuns* have been discovered at Tikal as well as many other sites. They are often several hundred cubic meters in size. Chultuns were used for storage of such foods as smoked or dried corn and ramón nuts, which were pounded into flour and baked in bread. Sometimes the porous walls of chultuns were plastered with powdered limestone and used as cisterns.

Above left: Stela 4 is a portrait in stone of the ninth ruler of Tikal, whom archaeologists have named Curl Nose because of the appearance of his name glyph. The stela, dedicated in A.D. 379, was discovered in 1904 by Teobert Maler, who found it standing on its head, placed that way by a little-known people who had resettled Tikal long after its fall.

Above right: Another portrait of Curl Nose, from a fragment of Stela 18 at Tikal, dedicated A.D. 396. About one-third of the stela was never found.

Above: Stela 32, which bears no date, has been described as a depiction of the Mexican rain god, Tlaloc. It was discovered in an Early Classic cache in front of the North Acropolis by the Tikal Project in 1961.

Below: Stormy Sky, the eleventh ruler of Tikal, wearing a necklace of vertebrae. The son of Curl Nose, he ruled Tikal from A.D. 426 to 457. Stela 31, the most famous stela found at Tikal, features 29 with 201 hieroglyphs carved on the back. It is in an excellent state of preservation, with the exception of the bottom part of the figure and several glyphs that were damaged by the Maya themselves.

Stela 1 at Tikal may be another depiction of Stormy Sky. An Early Classic stela, it bears a dedicatory date of circa A.D. 455 to 475. This is another figure with a string of vertebrae hanging on his body. At the bottom right, the Tikal glyph appears as a headdress for a long-nosed god.

The front of Stela 2, carved in the same style as Stela 1, is probably another depiction of Stormy Sky. Maler unearthed this upper part of Stela 2 while digging in Tikal's North Acropolis in search of the missing portion of Stela 1.

Above: Stela 26, left side, partial panel of glyphs. Stela 26 is known as the Red Stela because of the red paint that covered it when it was discovered, shattered, in a room in the North Acropolis at Tikal. The front may contain the figure of Jaguar Paw Skull II, another ruler of Tikal. The bottom right-hand glyph bears the Tikal emblem.

Below: Altar 14 was discovered in 1959 by the Tikal Project in Twin Pyramid Complex M. Tikal marked twenty-year periods, or katuns, with commemorative twin pyramid complexes, beginning with katun ten in A.D. 633. In its center, Altar 14 bears the only short-count date found at Tikal, a large glyph of Ahau, one of the Maya day glyphs, with a bar and three dots accompanying the glyph. Around the edge appears the long count, the equivalent of A.D. 692. Both the name glyph for Ah Cacau and the emblem glyph of Tikal appear on the altar.

Altar 5 from the Twin Pyramid Complex N. Many consider this carving to be the finest Maya work of art at Tikal. The accompanying Stela 16 bears the figure of Ah Cacau and a dedicatory date of A.D. 711. The four dates found in the band of glyphs surrounding the two figures on Altar 5 seem to have astronomical importance. The figure on the left brandishes an instrument called a chest opener, an object that originated in Mexico. The other figure holds a flint knife.

Above: Stela 21 at Tikal was found in 1951 in a shattered condition. This is glyphic text from the stone. Many parts of the figure on the stela—that of a ruler called Yaxkin Caan Chac—had been carried away by local people. One piece from the lower right was eventually recovered from a home a kilometer or so away, where the owner had fashioned it into a metate. The stela bears a dedicatory date of A.D. 736. The remaining glyphs and the foot of the figure testify to the exquisiteness of the carving. The upper left-hand glyph has the Tikal emblem carved in the form of an animal head.

Below: Detail of a carved foot with anklet from Stela 21.

Opposite: Stela 22 is the commemorative monument for Twin Pyramid Complex Q. It bears a dedicatory date of A.D. 771 and is a portrait of a ruler known as Chitam. The monument was discovered by Tikal Project director Edwin Shook in 1956, the first year of work at Tikal for the project. Complex Q is the largest of its kind at Tikal and the last of six twin pyramid complexes found there.

119

Above: Altar 7, located at the base of Temple III at Tikal. Badly fragmented, Altar 7 shows the head of a deity resting in a bowl with a woven mat alongside.

Below: Altar 8 accompanies Stela 20 in Tikal's Twin Pyramid Complex P. A bound, yet somehow graceful figure lies on an altar, probably awaiting execution. The Tikal emblem glyph adorns the head of a monster mask worked into the altar. Although eroded (perhaps damaged by the Maya), the intent look on the prisoner's face is still discernible.

Above: The smallest of three ball courts found at Tikal. This one is located alongside Temple I in the main plaza.
Below: A small, Classic-style stela that was found in front of Tikal's North Acropolis.

The most famous depiction at Tikal is known as the Dancer. It is found on an entrance wall at Maler's Palace in the Central Acropolis.

Text and a crouching figure with nose bone are featured on the side of Stela 20, erected in front of a small temple that served as an observatory at Uaxactun. Observatories are in the Maya lowlands. Stela 20 is facing due east, on an exact center line between the solstices and equinoxes determined by the front corners of the temple. The stone bears a date of A.D. 490.

Stela 26, also from Uaxactun, dated A.D. 445.

Unwanted by early looters, this fragment from a shattered stela at El Bejucal lay unmolested for centuries. A few months after this photograph was taken, the piece was missing.

123

Above: Looters tunneling into the side of the Templo del Diablo uncovered very fine masonry work and part of a stuccoed figure on the facade of the structure.

Below: Apparently considered worthless to the looters of El Zotz, faint hieroglyphs will yet yield information to patient epigraphers.

Opposite: The poor quality of this photograph results from its being a copy of a poor Polaroid image. It was given to me in the hope that I might know of a potential buyer for the monument. (I did not!) The seller wanted sixty thousand U.S. dollars, for which he would transport the stone any place within Guatemala. He would not say where the monument had been found. I have included the photograph to point out how organized gangs of looters can be capable of moving such a stone, probably weighing well over a ton, with seeming impunity.

Above: *El tigrillo,* a young margay, poses a fleeting instant for the camera. Many exotic animals of El Peten, long hunted for their hides, are now only glimpsed in the deepest parts of the forest. Although forbidden by law to hunt the animals, and despite a U.S. law prohibiting the importation of a spotted fur of any kind into the United States, poachers continue to supply skins to lucrative markets in other countries.

Below: Our party and several guardianes stand in the middle of a stela graveyard at El Peru. This was another site thoroughly looted before its existence became known to authorities.

Above: A long-nosed god, or chac, remains in the corner of a stela from which the main figure has been removed.

Below: This mask is from another shattered stela.

127

Above: Fragment from the monument grave-yard at El Peru.

Below: Sculpture signatures on a stela from El Peru.

Opposite above: The throne from Piedras Negras, with a monster back and Maya lords appearing in its eyes.

Opposite below: Piedras Negras reached its peak of sculptural brilliance in A.D. 761 with the completion of this small, exquisitely carved wall panel, or perhaps lintel, known as Wall Panel 3. On it, a hereditary chief called a *halach uinic* (seated lord) is holding council with lords (some of them from other sites). It is thought that this monument may have commemorated the choosing of a successor.

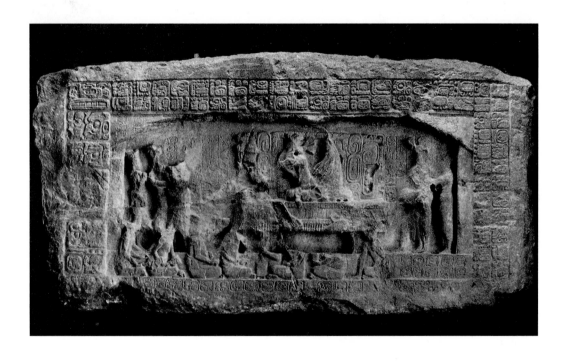

129

Above: Several prisoners bound with a common rope await their fate on Stela 12 from Piedras Negras. Notice the depiction of dejection and fear on their faces. Eight artists have signed their names to Stela 12.

Opposite: High on a limestone outcropping at San Diego, a carved figure dwarfs the men below.

Opposite: A close look at the cliff figure at San Diego.

Above: Abundant in the hot, dry part of the year, the scorpion, or *alacrán*, was sometimes the object of Maya art. The Indians say that if a person is stung before noon, the pain will ease by nightfall, allowing sleep. If stung in the afternoon, however, a victim will get no sleep that night. Here, a mother alacrán takes her brood with her on her daily rounds.

Below: Stela 2 from Polol, dedicated in A.D. 810. The artist who carved the figure seems to have run out of stone, necessitating a considerable shortening of its left arm.

Above: Artist Merle Greene Robertson records hieroglyphs on rice paper at the site of Itzan, using a technique called rubbing. We had the pleasure of outfitting and taking her to several Maya sites in the Sayaxche area, where she recorded stelae in the late sixties.

Below: Stela 4 from the small site of Itsimte. This is all of the fragmented stela that was found.

Opposite: This stela, found in fragments at Itzan, featured nothing but hieroglyphs. It held over two hundred glyphs, the largest stone message found in the Maya lowlands.

Above: On the front patio of the Hotel Cuyacan in the village of Sayaxche, I (slightly) assist explorer and archaeologist Ian Graham in putting together fragments of Stela 2. Graham, on the right, had supervised the hauling of all the remaining pieces of this stela from the site of La Amelia to Sayaxche.

Opposite: The puzzle completed, Stela 2 (re-erected in 1968) now stands proudly in front of the municipal building at Sayaxche. Notice the seemingly happy jaguar at the bottom.

137

138

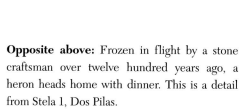

Opposite above: Frozen in flight by a stone craftsman over twelve hundred years ago, a heron heads home with dinner. This is a detail from Stela 1, Dos Pilas.

Opposite below: Known as El Emperador by local people, this Dos Pilas stela, referred to by archaeologists as Stela 16, is undated but Late Classic in style. The figure wearing a tubular beaded skirt is probably that of a woman.

Above left: In 1971, a gang of looters using stone saws cut up and carried away Stela 17 from Dos Pilas. An alert immigration officer at the seaport of Puerto Barrios became suspicious of *very* heavy suitcases. As a result, all but one piece of Stela 17 was recovered.

Above right: Lying where it had fallen, Stela 17 at Dos Pilas lay untouched for over a thousand years. This monument has a dedicatory date of A.D. 810.

Left: Other than having shattered when it toppled, Stela 2 at Dos Pilas is in a remarkable state of preservation. It stood close to fifteen feet tall and is dated A.D. 735.

Right: Hieroglyphic text from a stela discovered in 1977 at a site called Los Duendes. It is probably a satellite of Dos Pilas, just a few minutes' walk away. The emblem glyph of Tikal appears twice in the text, as the fourth glyph from the left in the top row and, more plainly, as the sixth glyph on the right in the fourth row.

Above: The Los Duendes figure accompanying the text wears an elaborate headdress-mask and, rather than a spear, carries a more peaceful manikin scepter in his hand.

Below: Los Duendes means The Dwarfs, and dwarfs appearing at the feet of a ruler carved on a monument there gave the small site its name. Dwarfs played a key role in the mythology of the Maya. They were the first creation of men. At the time of the Spanish conquest, the Maya believed that there had been three previous creations, all of them destroyed by floods sent by the gods. It was believed by the Maya that the old, deserted cities were built by dwarfs who held magical powers and were able to whistle the great blocks of stone into place. All of this activity took place in the dark, as there was no sun as yet. One group, the little men of the forest, fell into disfavor with the creators, who sent a great scorching sun to turn them into stone, thus explaining to Indians the small figures that are found at various ruins today.

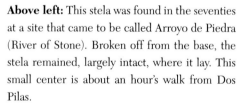

Above left: This stela was found in the seventies at a site that came to be called Arroyo de Piedra (River of Stone). Broken off from the base, the stela remained, largely intact, where it lay. This small center is about an hour's walk from Dos Pilas.

Above right: This stern-visaged figure from Arroyo de Piedra carries the familiar manikin scepter in one hand and clutches a small shield in the other. Carved in A.D. 731, the figure is said to be a vassal of a king from Dos Pilas. Many of the texts from stelae found around the Patixbatun area contain a reference to the great city of Tikal, which lay over a hundred kilometers to the northeast. The Tikal emblem glyph appears here as the sixth glyph on the right in the third row.

Opposite: Known locally as the Corn God, the figure on Stela 1 at Aguateca was traditionally thought to be scattering corn from his hand. Archaeologists have interpreted the figure to be a ruler shedding his own blood in an offering to Maya gods. The monument, dedicated in A.D. 741, is thought to commemorate a new ruler at Aguateca. The lower left-hand hieroglyph at the bottom is the emblem glyph of Aguateca.

Above: Parney VanKirk examines hieroglyphs from Stela 3 at Aguateca. This fine monument was kept from falling by the aid of an indio desnudo tree that grew alongside. The monument is no longer at Aguateca; its present location is unknown.

Below: The upper portion of Stela 1, Cancuen. There are recorded instances of victims being sacrificed in a standing position, fastened to stakes or other upright objects.

Above: Showing a great deal of so-called Mexican influence, this small, intricately carved stela is from the Maya site of Tres Islas.
Below: Small and beautifully carved, this ball-court marker was recovered from the ruins of Cancuen.

145

Stela 4, Machaquila.   Stela 3 from Machaquila, dedicated in A.D. 815.

Stela 7 from the site of Machaquila. No spears or shields were found on sculptures there. Instead, many of the rulers depicted carry a manikin scepter. Fortunately, the three stelae shown here were brought out of the remote site before looters overran it.

The missing piece of Seibal's Stela 9, reerected by Harvard University workers, was never found. Date glyphs on the stone were deciphered as A.D. 849.

Opposite: Stela 10 at Seibal is a superb example of Maya art, bearing a date of A.D. 849.

Above left: Stela 8 is another monument dated A.D. 849. This was a great year for stelae at Seibal. Four of the finely carved monuments were dedicated and set in place at the four sides of Temple A-3.

Above right: Seibal's Stela 11 also bears the date of A.D. 849. Archaeologists believe that the figures on Stelae 10 and 11 are the same.

Situated close to the Río Pasión and not far from the village of Sayaxche, the ruins at Seibal were for many years conveniently reached by means of the Pasión. The Pasión, Salinas, Usumacinta, Lacantun, and dozens of other rivers and arroyos served as highways for the Maya, and these rivers are still the most convenient way to travel for many people. Here a great dugout, called a *cayuco,* leaves Sayaxche to return to a village upriver. The villagers had come into town on a Saturday morning for supplies and a social get-together. This canoe was hollowed out of a single

mahogany tree, but today it is difficult, if not impossible, to find a mahogany tree anywhere near the size of the one that was used here. Dugout canoes are ordered from cayuco makers in specific measurements. For example, a small cayuco might be ordered with a ten-quintal capacity and another to hold thirty. (A quintal is a unit of weight equaling one hundred pounds.) The price of the dugout varies with the amount it will hold. We once owned a dugout forty-three feet in length. It was supposedly a hundred-quintal canoe. It held fifty people with ease.

Above: A visitor often asks a local Indian if a certain figure on a stela has a name. The person asked might cast a glance at the stone in question; if there is an apparent motif, it has an inordinate influence on the answer. Stela 19 at Seibal, shown here, was believed to depict corn being scattered about. This gave rise to the stela figure's name of Yum Kaax, for the Maya corn god. Modern archaeologists believe the figure is scattering blood in ritual sacrifice, but local Indians still think it is corn.

Right: Artist Merle Greene Robertson calls Stela 3 from Seibal "one of the great masterpieces of Seibal sculpture." Mexican influence is apparent in the carving.

Above: The text from Stela 19 at Seibal, Late Classic in style and assigned a date of around A.D. 870.

Below: Erected about A.D. 780, the figure on Seibal's Stela 7 wears a chest girdle or yoke and a kneepad, often accoutrements of Maya ballplayers.

Of the more than fifty carved monuments found at Seibal, Stela 13 is certainly the most unusual. The five serpents wrapped about the figure are fer-de-lances (barba amarillas), one of the world's most dangerous snakes.

Of Stela 1 at Seibal, archaeologist John Graham wrote, "A clear premonition of coming decadence is to be observed. Although the sculpture is of considerable artistic merit, the carving is notably broader and cruder in execution than monuments dating only twenty years earlier at Seibal." This stone carving was dedicated in A.D. 869. It was one of the last monuments erected at Seibal.

Above left: Stela 14 stands marking a causeway that leads to an outlying group of buildings at Seibal.

Above right: A very late stela from Seibal.

Opposite above: Reconstructed by Harvard's Peabody Museum in the mid-sixties, this small in-the-round structure at Seibal was probably a viewing stand, possibly for spectators of sacrifices carried out on the jaguar table in front.

Opposite below: Small jaguar table in front of the circular structure at Seibal. The weight-bearing column at the center was placed by Harvard Expedition members. The table was originally held up by the three figures crouching beneath.

El tigre, the mighty jaguar, monarch of the jungle, was held in great respect by the Maya. It was the subject of countless Maya ceremonies, appears on murals, bowls, vases, plates, and is depicted in figures of jade and clay. A jaguar god was the patron of number seven. He was also the lord of the Maya day Akbal. Once plentiful, jaguars are almost gone from the fast-disappearing jungles of El Peten. Severe hunting and the destruction of their habitat have made them a rarity in the wild. This great beast, which the Indians refer to as *muy noble,* is the world's third largest feline and the New World's largest.

Above right: Hieroglyphs from a stela segment adorning temple steps at Seibal.

Opposite: As is the case with so many discoveries, the cave at Canchecan was brought to light when a campesino cleared a field to plant corn using an age-old method of slashing and burning. Inside the small grotto, five burials had taken place. Over each of the burials, a face was carved into the limestone stalagmite. Any artifacts that may have accompanied the persons interred had been removed.

 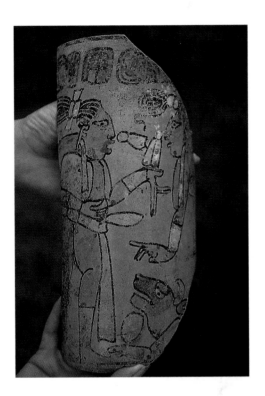

An extremely well-contrived whistle, still bearing the original paint, was discovered deep in a cave close to the town of Poptun. There are thousands of unexplored caves in the Maya Mountains that border the Maya lowlands on the east side of El Peten. New discoveries are frequently made. Unfortunately, by the time responsible authorities learn of these discoveries, many caves have been thoroughly looted.

Above right: This beautiful piece from a vase was found in an unnamed cave near the town of Poptun in El Peten. Strangely, no other piece of the vessel was found. It was perhaps dropped, and remained unnoticed by looters.

Opposite: Stretching over seventy meters at its broadest point, the first great chamber of Naj Tunich is referred to as the Main Entrance Hall. Its ceiling is some thirty feet high. At one end of this enormous cavern, a balcony was created using retaining walls and fill. It was built during Early Classic times, A.D. 250 to 550.

Above: Known as a *coche de monte* by the Indians, a collared peccary darts through a patch of sunlight. Traveling in packs and very numerous in the deep woods of El Peten, this wild pig is a source of meat for today's hunters as it no doubt was for the ancient Maya. A hoary bush tale relates that if a pack of coche come across their mortal enemy, the jaguar, they attack instantly with a ferociousness that drives the great cat into the nearest tree. At this, all the coche immediately urinate at the base of the tree. So strong is the odor that the jaguar is overcome, passes out, and falls from the tree, to be dispatched by the waiting sharp tusks of the wild pigs. It was just such a wild pig as this that Don Emilio Pop wounded on the day he discovered Naj Tunich.

Below: The first archaeologists to excavate and study Naj Tunich were James and Sandra Brady, shown here examining artifacts brought from the cave in 1982.

A

B

A–F. Carved on a blue grey slatelike stone, the Classic hieroglyphs on this and the following two pages are from a fallen and fragmented stela at Sacul. When we visited there and took these photos in the early eighties, the fragmented stela was awaiting transportation to an unknown destination. This monument bears a dedicatory date of A.D. 761.

C

D

E

F

Carved for an eternity, Stela 1. From the ruins of
Ixtutz.

Stela 1 at Ixkun, dated A.D. 790, is certainly one
of the most ambitious monuments carved by the
Maya. Four meters high, it is the tallest standing
monument in the Maya lowland area. A unique
feature of this monolith are the four holes drilled
into each side. Early archaeologist Sylvanus Morley suggested that "the holes may have held
torches in some on-going ceremony."

164

This eroded figure on a large stela at El Chal is
nearly all that remains after centuries of exposure
to the hot, wet climate of El Peten.

Although badly eroded, a portion of hieroglyphic
text from a monument at El Chal may still yield
information to archaeologists.

Above: Wooden beams that spanned the inner doorways of the palace at Tzikin Tzakan. The outer chamber had collapsed earlier. The wood of the beams comes from the *sapodilla*, the tree from which *chicleros* gather sap to be used in chewing gum. Sapodilla wood is extremely hard, and boring insects do not seem to be attracted to it, which accounts for the beams' being in place after a thousand years. The whole structure is now a huge pile of debris.

Below: To give perspective, a local man posed within the partially fallen arch of a palace at Tzikin Tzakan. This great building fell in completely during the heavy rains of 1980. When intact, its length was over one hundred feet, the longest of any Maya building.

Above left: Slaked lime, or *cal*, has been manufactured in the same way for many centuries by the Maya and their descendants. Natural chunks of limestone are fired in *caleras* like this one. After it is cooled, the white powder that remains serves many purposes, ranging from plaster and paint to lime water in which corn is soaked overnight. (The next morning the corn is removed from the hull and ground into dough for the day's tortillas.)

Above right: A temple roof comb rises above the jungle canopy at Río Azul. Despite extensive damage done by an army of looters, excavations there revealed a great deal of information.

Opposite above: Parney VanKirk leaves a tomb at Río Azul that has been looted. I confess to extreme nervousness during the short time I subsequently spent in the tomb. Parney and I had reasoned that she would be the first one in whenever one of these tight spots was to be investigated. We thought that, because she weighed very little, I would be better equipped to get her out of any trouble than she would me if something happened. Fortunately, we never had to test our theory, although sometimes our Indian companions would give me strange looks as I lowered my wife into some hole or other.

Opposite below: The tomb of a ruler whom archaeologists have named simply Ruler X. The date series in the central panel reads September 27, A.D. 416. Looters had broken into this Río Azul tomb a week before our visit.

The roof comb of Temple 216 at Yaxcha pokes through the jungle canopy. This is the tallest structure at the site.

Above: Lake Macanche in El Peten. Except for the addition of electricity to this small village, daily life is carried on today much as it was in the days of the ancient Maya. Steel machetes have replaced flint-edged cutting tools, and the people now use shotguns instead of bows, arrows, and spears. Old gods are still revered, however, and turkeys are sacrificed to them on important occasions, such as the planting of a milpa. A pointed, fire-hardened pole called a dibble stick, whose origin is as old as the ancient Maya themselves, is still the preferred tool for planting corn. The stick is pushed into the earth a prescribed depth, then several kernels of corn are dropped into the hole and covered with dirt tamped down by foot.

Below: This group of men build a shelter, using leaves from the *corrozo* palm found in the jungle. Every part, pole and thatch, has a specific name and place for the builders. The method used in building a dwelling like this has not changed throughout centuries.

Above: A stuccoed rain god, or *chac,* looks out from the front of the Temple of the Masks, located in the center of the North Acropolis at Tikal.

Below: In the Tikal National Park, everything enjoys protection—animals and plants as well as the ruins. Penalties for infractions can be costly. The wildlife of the region quickly took advantage of this afforded protection, and many species now live in harmony with the thousands of yearly visitors. This boat-billed heron peers pontifically from her nest at the Tikal *aguada* (water hole).

Opposite: One of two massive stuccoed masks discovered by excavators deep in Tikal's North Acropolis. This great mask adorned an earlier temple.

Above: The recently excavated and restored Great Pyramid in the Lost World Complex is the largest building, in mass, at Tikal.

Opposite: Stela 9 shows Tikal ruler Kan Boar in all his finery. The monument bears a dedicatory date of A.D. 475. It is not clear whether Kan Boar was the twelfth or thirteenth ruler of Tikal.

174

A glyph panel from the left side of Stela 5 at
Tikal. The front of the stela bears the figure of
Yaxkin Caan Chac, the twenty-seventh ruler of
Tikal. The dedicatory date of Stela 5 is A.D. 744.

The commemorative Stela 20 from the Twin Pyramid Complex P has a dedicatory date of A.D. 751 and is possibly a portrait of Yaxkin Caan Chac. It was discovered by Edwin Shook in 1937. Like all the monuments photographed at Tikal that appear in this book, this is a photo of the original stela. It has been the practice of the Guatemalan government to remove the originals from Tikal in order to better protect them, replacing them with cement replicas. Few if any of the original monuments remain in situ. Notice the happy little jaguar on the bottom of the stone.

The chamber in one of the great palaces at Uaxactun. Height of rooms was not much of a problem for Maya architects; however, the inherent
problems of a corbel-arched room dictated nar-
rowness. Around nine feet seemed to be the max-
imum width the Maya were able to achieve.

Constructed around A.D. 250, this small temple at Uaxactun was one of the earliest ever found in the Maya lowlands. Excavated in 1974 from beneath another construction, it emerged a gleaming white from the stucco plaster with which it had been covered. The decades during which it has lain exposed have not been kind. Rains and a hot, humid climate have removed most of the stucco. The twelve large jaguar-god masks that adorn the building are, for the most part, undiscernible.

A small, debris-covered mound at El Bejucal.
This time the looters were frustrated, as the tunnel led to nothing.

No Indian goes hungry or thirsty anytime in El Peten. The jungle provides food and water. I once watched an old Indian poke a stick into an animal burrow. (If mosquitoes emerge when this is done, an animal such as a paca [*tepeizcuintli*] or an armadillo [*geüche*] is at home.) The man then slowly thrust a sharpened stake several times through the top of the burrow. Upon feeling movement, he quickly struck the stick a heavy blow with a rock, pinning the unfortunate animal. The prey, a paca, was then dug out and roasted on a crude wooden frame over coals. The meat was delicious. Water can always be found in tree stumps, in pools left when rivers dry up, or from a unique vine, the *bejuco de agua*. When a three- or four-foot section of this water vine is cut at an angle and held to the mouth, it yields cool, sweet water. The site of El Bejucal is famous for an abundance of this vine. Chicleros often fill a fifty-gallon drum with water from the vine in very little time.

Opposite: All that is left of a wonderfully carved stela at San José de Motul, accidently destroyed by fire when an old man cleared and burned a field in preparation for planting his milpa.

Above: This fallen and broken stela at Motul awaits an archaeologist. In the meantime, the jungle slowly has its way with the stone. In this inhospitable hot, wet climate, nothing is impervious.

At the ruins of La Florida (Ocultun), Stela 9 lies in a cleared field just off the Aviateca grass airstrip. Most of the hieroglyphs on this monument have been cut off and spirited away. The face of the figure shown was probably destroyed by the Maya themselves.

Elaborate pains were taken, including building this none-too-stable ladder, in order to photograph the figure carved on the face of this cliff at San Diego.

The chamber at the top of the great pyramid at
Polol, with floors ripped up by thieves in search
of artifacts.

The hieroglyphic stairway leading to the top of a
pyramid at Dos Pilas before it was cleared in the
early nineties by a group of scientists under the
direction of Vanderbilt University.

Above: Bound prisoners carved on the stone used in steps are a common theme throughout the Patixbatun area. This step is from Dos Pilas. **Below:** With a half-smile on its face, this small head lay among the ruins at Dos Pilas, of no particular interest to anyone. Shortly after the artifact craze hit Guatemala, the stone was missing.

Above: This section of a stone stairway at Tamarandito shows a bound prisoner and glyphs that perhaps contain his name.

Below: An amazing mimic, the banjo head leaf mantis blends incredibly with the broad leaf on which it is resting. One cannot help but wonder whether the ancient Maya came to recognize the beneficial aspects of this great killer. Pound for pound, the mantis is one of the greatest hunters on earth, each day devouring as much as five times its own weight in other insects, including mosquitoes.

Opposite: Dedicated in A.D. 735, Stela 2 at Aguateca bears the same ruler figure carved on Stela 2 at nearby Dos Pilas. Aguateca is thought to be the fortress city built by a prince of a Tikal dynasty during a time of heavy warfare. Defeated at Dos Pilas, the inhabitants fled to Aguateca, just a few miles away. This strategy seems not to have worked, as Aguateca was terminally overrun in the mid-ninth century.

Above: Here we are following the banks of the Río Machaquila on our way to the ruins of the same name. There was no trail and not much of a river at this dry time of year.

Below: On reaching Machaquila, our party found nothing but desolation. Great altars had been shattered; stelae left at the site had become victims of rock saws. Pits and tunnels scarred pyramids and palaces.

Above left: Friend and guide, guardián Don Dacio Castillo, examines the graveyard of monuments at Machaquila.

Above right: Although well fashioned, this piece, probably some form of tenon, was not ornate enough to justify carrying it away. Now, however, even a simple piece such as this would not be left behind.

Opposite: Parney VanKirk takes time to examine the wonderful stonework of ancient architects at Machaquila.

192

It would be difficult to imagine a more beautiful jungle setting than that surrounding the ruins of Seibal, which has been partially reconstructed by the Harvard University's Peabody Museum. Thanks to the ongoing efforts of the Guatemalan government, the grounds and trails at Seibal are kept immaculate and have a lovely, parklike quality. This small ceremonial temple sits in the middle of a large plaza. Dozens of great pyramids still remain covered and choked with brush, awaiting the trowels and computers of future archaeologists.

194

Above: The fer-de-lance, or *barba amarilla* (yellow beard) to the Indians, this snake gets its name from the yellowish cast on the underside of its jaw. This pit viper is justly feared by nearly everyone. It is also called the ten-step snake. (The inference is obvious.) The fangs of the barba are long, and the amount of venom injected copious. The bite, unless immediate help is at hand, often proves fatal. This reptile was held in awe by the Maya—and is by anyone else with any sense!

Below: Stela 2 at Seibal was described by Sylvanus Morley as being "masked by the flayed face of a victim." Eric Thompson thought the figure might represent the Mexican "unpleasant god of flaying, Xipe Totec."

Wonderfully carved glyphs from a stela fragment
at Seibal. The bottom glyph is the emblem of
Seibal.

CHAPTER THREE

THE HIGHLANDS

KAMINALJUYU (HILLS OF THE DEAD)

The great valley of Guatemala, rich and fertile with volcanic soil 'and blessed with abundant rainfall and temperate climate, has long been attractive to settlers. Thirty-three known Maya sites nestle in this valley alone, the most important one being Kaminaljuyu.

The Carnegie Institute worked at Kaminaljuyu in the 1930s and 1940s and the University of Pennsylvania in the 1960s. These organizations recorded over two hundred mounds and thirteen ball courts.

Kaminaljuyu was occupied as early as 850 B.C., with a population of over fifty thousand people. Maya art, evidenced in sculptures and ceramics, reached a higher level at Kaminaljuyu than at any other Highland Maya center. Strangely, after centuries of apparent prosperity and growth, this great city fell into virtual ruin between the third and fourth century A.D. This was not the end, however. Mexican invaders from the far northern city of Teotihuacan occupied Kaminaljuyu and built for themselves a miniature version of their own great city. There began a tremendous period of growth and far-reaching influence for the people of Kaminaljuyu.

For excavators, the most exciting finds were sumptuous burials contained within mounds. Custom at Kaminaljuyu was to bury a ruler, priest, lord, or other dignitary in a seated position. The dead were accompanied by articles that they would need in the next world: superb carved jades, intricately painted bowls and other vessels, weapons, and food. Often, sacrificed slaves were buried with an important person, so that they might also serve their master in another world.

Workshops where artisans fashioned jades and obsidian were also found at Kaminaljuyu, indicating that it was an important trade center.

Today most of this great Maya city lies beneath the sprawling urban housing developments of Guatemala City. There is very little left to remind one of its glorious past. The only echoes one hears are of blaring horns from traffic on nearby bustling Roosevelt Highway.

The construction of modern houses on the site—every basement dug yielded up treasures—gave birth to an instant cottage industry, trafficking in antiquities. During the 1970s, few tourists could visit the site without being approached by a local offering an artifact for just a few dollars. Objects proffered ranged from small clay heads called *muñecas* to jades and vases that would command many hundreds of dollars with collectors.

K'UMARCAAJ (PLACE OF THE ROTTEN REEDS), FORMERLY UTATLAN (PLACE OF THE CANE FIELDS)

During the Spanish conquest of Guatemala in the 1500s, Mexican Indian allies of Pedro Alvarado established the habit of giving subdued cities a Mexican interpretation of existing Maya names. Hence K'umarcaaj, Maya Quiche for Rotten Reed, became Utatlan, Nahuatl for Place of the Cane Fields. It is now again called by its former Maya name. This was the capital for the most powerful Maya tribe in the highlands, the Quiche. It was also one of the oldest Maya centers in the highlands.

At the time of the conquest many highland cities, convinced of the invincibility of the Spaniards, sought to appease the invaders with offers of vassals and gifts. Not so K'umarcaaj; it decided to fight. It was to no avail.

A decisive battle was waged between the Spanish and their allies against nearly nine thousand warriors from K'umarcaaj. The Spanish triumphed and, in the process, killed the great Maya war chief Tecun Uman. In a desperate attempt to rid themselves of the Spanish, K'umarcaaj turned to deception. Alvarado was invited into K'umarcaaj ostensibly to discuss terms of surrender with the rulers. The Maya town was situated on a high, small plain, surrounded on three sides by untraversable ravines and with only a causeway leading into the city. An overheard conversation, quickly related to Alvarado, saved the Spanish from possible death. The rulers had sent the women and children to safety and commanded that all houses be filled with dry wood. Once the Spanish were inside the town, the causeway was to be destroyed, buildings fired, and the hated Spanish done away with.

Alvarado, upon hearing of the plot, made immediate plans to leave. The chiefs begged him to stay the night, but the wily commander explained that his horses were supernatural beings and could never spend a night within walls. Alvarado arrested several of the chiefs, bound them, and rode as fast as possible over the causeway to safety. It had been so close, Alvarado explained in a letter to Hernán Cortés, that the causeway had all but been destroyed and he and his men had experienced "great difficulty" in leaving. The Spanish lost one man to arrows during the episode.

The next day, the captured lords of K'umarcaaj were burned alive by Alvarado. It took the Spanish and their allies several more battles before the Quiche capitulated. Alvarado burned the town and sent most of its survivors into a life of slavery. It is perhaps fortunate that there were any survivors. Here is what Fray Bartolomé de Las Casas, a solid proponent of nonviolence (and in an extraordinary minority), had to say: "From the year 1518 until today which is 1542 has swelled up and come to a head all the wickedness, injustice, violence and tyranny which the Christians have done in the Indies. . . . I affirm it as very certain and approved that during these forty years owing to the aforesaid tyrannies and infernal works of the Christians

more than twelve million souls, men, women, and children have perished unjustly and tyrannically; and in truth I would not be overstepping the mark in saying fifteen million." This last figure is only a little less than the number of people in Guatemala today.

Shortly thereafter, in a camp on the plains outside K'umarcaaj, a daughter was born to Alvarado and his Tlaxcalan Indian wife Doña Louisa Xicotencatl. Named Leanora, the child was the first mestiza born in Guatemala.

By killing the great war chief Tecun Uman, Alvarado guaranteed the man a measure of immortality. In countless villages and towns throughout Guatemala, in fiestas and on religious days, Tecun Uman and Pedro Alvarado enter into endless combat in the Dance of the Conquistadors. Tecun Uman is a revered hero, Alvarado a despised tyrant.

The quiet, grass-covered mounds of K'umarcaaj are still held in reverence by thousands of Indians in the surrounding area. Descendants of ancient royal houses from K'umarcaaj can be traced to families that now live in the nearby town of Santa Cruz del Quiche.

Iximche (Corn Tree)

Iximche is one of the most beautiful Maya sites to be found in the Guatemalan highlands. The ruins are situated some eighty-five kilometers west of Guatemala City, close to the town of Tecpan. Iximche was the last capital for the Cakchiquel Maya. This group, once under the yoke of the Quiche

Maya, broke away and founded their own hastily built city about A.D. 1470. Their chosen site was one of defense, on a level plateau nearly surrounded by steep ravines.

In 1524 the Cakchiquel people were in trouble. Facing revolt and further war with the Quiches and ravaged with plague (a gift of the Spanish), the Cakchiquel king sent to Pedro Alvarado for help. It was a fatal request. Alvarado came and eventually destroyed Iximche.

An early visitor to Iximche in 1690 wrote:

The city covered a plain from north to south and two miles east to west, which could be entered only through a very narrow causeway which was closed off by two doors of obsidian stone. The ground was covered by a thick layer of mortar. At one end could be seen the remains of a magnificent building perfectly square, on the sides of which might be seen traces of a sumptuous palace. Old foundations of houses could be seen surrounding the ceremonial center. The city was divided by a moat three yards deep, which ran from north to south and had battlements of rough stone and mortar more than a yard high. On the eastern side of the moat were the houses of the nobles and on the western side those of the common people. The streets were wide and straight. To the west could be seen a little hill which dominated the city, and on its summit might be observed the remains of a round building like the curb-stones of a well. . . . This

was the place where judges tried civil and criminal cases.

Alvarado was to use Iximche for his capital for a short time before burning it to the ground.

Iximche remains a sacred place and rallying point for the Cakchiquels. As recently as February 1980, the Indians issued what has come to be known as the Declaration of Iximche:

We the indigenous peoples of Guatemala declare and denounce before the world: more than four centuries of discrimination, denial, repression, exploitation and massacres committed by the foreign invaders and continued by their most savage and criminal descendants to the present day. . . . The massacre at the Spanish embassy is not an isolated case but part of a chain of killings. The suffering of our people has come down through the centuries, since 1524, when there arrived in these lands the assassin and criminal Pedro Alvarado.

In early 1980 government troops and police, learning that several Indian leaders were conferring with the ambassador of Spain, burned the building in a assault, killing all but the ambassador.

Even before the Spanish came, Iximche seems to have been a place of strife. Excavations carried out there in 1965 and 1968 turned up ten square yards of ground paved with the skulls of forty-eight humans sacrificially decapitated. An altar with a stone block and a flint ceremonial knife were also found, indicating to scientists that heart-removal sacrifice was also carried on. Still another form of ritual sacrifice may have been practiced at Iximche. A large stone altar, twelve feet in diameter, lay in the center of a plaza there. A similarity can be seen to those altars found in Aztec centers and known to be part of a ritual of gladiator sacrifice. In this type of sacrifice, a prisoner was carefully weakened, usually by starvation. The prisoner was then fastened in some way on top of the altar. He was given a weapon, a wooden blade edged with feathers. A warrior was chosen to fight the prisoner; *his* wooden blade, however, was edged with razor-sharp obsidian. The outcome was seldom in doubt. However, it seems that if the prisoner showed extreme courage against these terrible odds, he was sometimes set free (at least by the Aztecs).

An elite tomb that was discovered at Iximche yielded a rare cache of gold that included a crown. The entombed noble had been sent upon his journey into the underworld accompanied by three sacrificed victims.

For years after Iximche's demise, huge amounts of stonework were hauled away to the nearby town of Tecpan, where it was used in construction of buildings, many of which are still standing.

Zaculeu (White Earth)

Zaculeu is a small site—just over three acres—established around A.D. 600 and enduring until 1525, when it suffered the Spanish mailed fist. For nearly a thousand years, it was the capital of the Mam Maya.

Zaculeu rests on a small plain about six thousand feet above sea level in the shadow of the Cuchumatanes, Guatemala's highest mountain range. Exploration and restoration of the ruins of Zaculeu in the mid-1940s was sponsored by the United Fruit Company.

Temples and palaces were constructed with huge stone slabs thickly covered with limestone plaster. Noticeable by its absence throughout the highlands is the famed corbeled arch. One supposes the main reason for this to be the earthquakes that continually shake these mountains. Temples at Zaculeu, as well as at other highland sites, were flat-roofed, often constructed using beams covered by thatch or mortar.

Scientists were interested to discover that skeletons recovered from tombs at Zaculeu were appreciably shorter in stature than those of their jungle cousins.

The task of subduing Zaculeu was given by Pedro Alvarado to his brother Gonzales. The excuse given for this aggression was that Kaibil Balam (Two Jaguars), king of Zaculeu, had been part of the plot to burn the Spaniards at K'umarcaaj. Gonzales Alvarado set out from Iximche with a cavalry troop of forty horses, eighty experienced Spanish foot soldiers, and some two thousand Mexican and Maya allies. The siege of Zaculeu was long and bloody, finally ending after six weeks of fighting. At the end, both sides were suffering starvation. When a relief column with food arrived for the Spanish, it turned the tide in their favor.

As an odd footnote to history, the name of Kaibil, considered to have been a great warrior, was applied to a modern elite counterinsurgency battalion that is comprised of nearly all Ladinos. This unit is universally feared and hated by the Indian population.

Most Maya sites in the highlands have escaped heavy looting. The reasons? There were very few carved monuments at these late sites, and nothing apparent to steal. Further, many of these old cities were built in open areas with no surrounding jungle to mask activity. Perhaps most important of all, many of these ruins remain sacred to the Maya. Rites and rituals are still carried on there. Punishment to violators of sacred grounds is often swift and sometimes final.

MIXCO VIEJO (OLD PLACE OF CLOUDS)

Alvarado realized that his conquest would not be complete until he had brought the Pokomam Maya and their capital, Mixco Viejo, under his thumb. The task proved so difficult that a Spanish chronicler described it as one of the most daring undertakings of the conquistadors.

Mixco Viejo sits on a high ridge, surrounded by steep ravines called *barrancos*. The fortress capital proved almost impossible to assault. Where the sides of natural obstacles were not sufficiently steep and difficult to scale, the Maya gave nature a hand with excavations and bulwarks. There were enough dwellings in this fortress to house several thousand people.

Alvarado began by sending a company of men to attack the town, but they were driven off with heavy losses. Alvarado himself led the next assault. (His courage was never questioned, only his cruelty.) Again the Spanish were repelled. During this retreat they were attacked by a relief column of Maya warriors from Chinautla. A savage battle ensued with the issue in doubt for the better part of the day. The Spanish and their allies finally carried the battle, and from captured prisoners learned of a secret passage that would allow chieftains, nobles, and other important persons to escape if their hilltop fortress were breached.

Alvarado devised a method that finally worked. Using pairs of musketeers and crossbowmen, with each two men being protected from the spears, darts, and arrows of the defenders by a third man holding a shield over their heads, the Spanish worked their way up the torturous incline and finally entered and conquered Mixco Viejo. The people who had planned to escape in such a situation were captured as they entered a no-longer-secret passage.

Despite their being armed with much superior weapons, it had taken the conquistadors over a month to defeat the Maya of Mixco Viejo. Alvarado, fearing the town and its gallant defense might prove a rallying point in the future, sacked and burned Mixco Viejo. He forced the survivors to march forty miles away, where they founded a new village under the watchful eyes of their new masters. Except for the Itza Maya with their stronghold on the island of Tayasal in Lake Peten Itza, who would remain unconquered until 1697, the Maya as an independent and self governing people were finished.

MAXIMON, OR SAN SIMONE, JUDAS

At the end of a Maya year, there was (and is) a five-day period dreaded as a time of evil and bad luck. To help them through these unpropitious times, the ancient Maya had a revered god whom they called Mam (grandfather). Mam was honored with gifts and offerings during this bad period of time. His importance seemed to diminish with each passing day until the fifth day, when he was discarded, not to reappear until the time of bad luck came again the following year. Of all the things that have come to us from the ancient Maya, Mam is one of the most interesting.

Adorados (worshipers) have given Mam many names, such as Maximon (the most common), San Pedro, San Andres, San Miguel, San Jude, Judas Iscariot, and even Don Pedro Alvarado. After the conquest the Maya were never reluctant to incorporate Christian doctrine into their rituals, particularly if they thought it would prove beneficial.

Michael Mendelson wrote a description of one of the present-day Maximons:

Maximon is, basically, a flat piece of wood about two and one-half feet high and 6–8 inches thick. A little jar or enameled iron cup is strapped to the top end and contains the base of another piece of wood, or possibly a gourd which forms the core of the head. At the bottom end two jars contain the wooden legs. . . . When dressed for fiestas, the core is wrapped in rags and corn husks, held together with string and fitted with boots. An ajkun (native priest) covers the resultant bundle with two or three sets of clothes offered by Atitecos (the people of Santiago Atatlan) and pilgrims from other villages. A doll emerges, some four and one-half feet tall, clothed in shirt, belt and pants of Atiteco style plus a Texan 55-size hat, a blue serge jacket and a bib made of some 30 silk scarves. A crude wooden mask covers the head core."

In the small pueblo of San Andres Iztapa, close to Antigua, Guatemala, another Maximon exists. This one, a life-sized and lifelike manikin, resides in a modern brick temple constructed in the latter part of 1975. In the devastating earthquake of 1976, most of Iztapa was leveled. Maximon's temple, however, was literally unscathed. Not a window was broken! Needless to say, this has done nothing to impair the image of Maximon.

Above: Evidence of a once-great city slowly emerges from beneath mounds at Kaminaljuyu. The site is said to be a copy of the Mexican city of Teotihuacan, which seems to have had enormous influence on many Maya centers in Guatemala.

Below: This snarling, stylized jaguar adorns the side of a small altar from Kaminaljuyu. At least one authority has suggested that the round, flat stones we call altars were thrones on which nobles sat and gave audience.

Toad altar, carved from basalt at Kaminaljuyu. The curls at the mouth are characteristic of the mouths of Maya solar deities. It is thought that the curls on the toad represent the final stage of molting, during which the animal eats his discarded skin, thus signifying renewal or rebirth.

Left: Extraordinary in its design and artful execution, Stela 11 was found at Kaminaljuyu. A face with Mexican features can be seen behind the mask. This monument was carved from basalt, a material found in abundance there due to the many eruptions of nearby volcanoes. Archaeologist S. W. Miles wrote that, "although probably religious, little respect was shown monuments, particularly at Kaminaljuyú. They were smashed and scattered, re-used as foundation or paving or thrown into dumps. Only rarely were stelae or fragments carefully buried."

Right: Volcan Fuego, dormant for years, erupts in 1976, probably shaken into activity by the enormous and deadly earthquake that ravaged the highlands of Guatemala the same year. This earthquake was the greatest natural disaster in the entire written history of the North American continent in terms of the number of dead (fifty thousand) and homes destroyed (over one million).

The pyramid of Tohil at K'umarcaaj (Rotten Cane), renamed Utatlan by Aztec mercenaries with the Spanish conquistadors. The outer covering of stonework was removed after the Quiche Maya were defeated and reused to construct buildings in the nearby town of Santa Cruz del Quiche. K'umarcaaj is a very holy place to the Quiche Maya of today. Offertory fires and the burning of pom are conducted in the small, soot-blackened opening in the front of the pyramid.

Opposite above: The earthquake that struck Guatemala in the early morning hours of February 4, 1976, measured 7.6 on the Richter scale. The devastation was terrible. The Indian town of Tecpan was almost totally leveled.

Opposite below: It has been said that every square inch of arable land is utilized in the Guatemalan highlands. Each section shown here is probably owned by a different family. We were told a story by an old Indian from the town of Nahuala who related, with a completely deadpan face, how a campesino had been killed falling *out* of—or off of—his cornfield. It seems that he had planted corn on a very steep hillside, almost a chasm; to work in his milpa he found it necessary to secure himself to a handy tree with a rope as a safety line. This method worked for years until the unfortunate day the frayed rope broke and the unlucky man tumbled to his death.

Above left: Yum Kaax, the Maya god of corn. The figurine was made from a mold that had probably formed hundreds of this effigy.

Above right: With early morning light pouring into her home, a Cakchiquel matron prepares dough from corn for the day's tortillas. With electricity now in most villages, corn-grinding machines have replaced manos and metates. Old-timers, however, complain about this modern method, claiming that they cannot taste the stone.

209

Opposite above: The largest temple at Zaculeu, restored by the United Fruit Company. Square columns at the top once supported wooden beams, which were probably roofed over with palm thatch.

Opposite below: This small temple at Zaculeu looks Roman in its construction. Note the barrel columns at both sides of the temple; they once supported wooden beams and thatched roofs.

Above: The ruins of Cahyup sit on top of a very tall hill overlooking the Rabinal valley.

Above: From the palace at Cahyup the view of the fertile Rabinal valley stretches out far below. When we visited this site in the troubled eighties, I first paid a call on the local army commander. When I asked the captain if we had anything to worry about, he replied: "Only if I catch you out there without Guatemalan papers. If I do, I shoot you." We checked our papers. We had another bad moment when a government fighter plane began buzzing us while we were at the top. Fortunately, after we had spent ten minutes or so trying to keep the palace between him and us, he flew off.

Opposite: The fortress site of Mixco Viejo proved extremely difficult for the Spanish conquistadors to overcome. With the fall of Mixco Viejo, the Maya lost their independence and way of life and were thrust into a subservience from which many say they have never escaped.

This structure, with its superb stonework, was
probably a viewing stand for the Maya of Mixco
Viejo. Totally destroyed in the earthquake of
1976, it has since been reconstructed by the
Guatemalan government.

Huts in the village of Tzutuhil at Lake Atitlan.
Life there remains virtually unchanged from that
of the villagers' ancestors.

Above: His work finished for the day, a Mam Indian living near the mountain village of Todos Santos heads for the steam bath his wife will have prepared by heating stones over which water will be poured. Rivers in the highlands tend to be very cold and are not much favored for baths. The modern Maya are an extremely clean people, most bathing in some form every day.

Opposite: For centuries trees have been felled without regard to future needs. The situation is presently so critical that felling trees is prohibited in some parts of the highlands. Even where cutting trees is permitted, a *lañero* (woodcutter) must often travel miles before finding a tree worthy of cutting. Most of the wood that is cut is used in cooking fires.

Above: Changing ways. A young woman from Potzun travels home with her jug of water from the town *pila* (water fountain). Plastic jugs have replaced traditional fired clay jugs in most of Guatemala. Not only are they cheaper and lighter in weight, but they seldom break when accidentally dropped.

Opposite: Some ways never change, as evidenced by this thousand-year-old figurine.

219

Above: Tribal leaders from the Maya Quiche tribe arrive at the Catholic church in Chichicastenango to attend mass. Silver sunbursts on staffs are symbols of authority.

Below: Mostly loyal to Christianity in some form, Indians often slip quietly away to worship old gods in old ways. Here, an elder offers pom and prayers to one of the old gods in the hills close to the town of Chichicastenango.

An elder from the village of Solola, close to Lake Atitlan, knows progress in a new pair of plastic shoes. These *zapatos plásticos* can be manufactured and sold more cheaply than shoes made of leather.

With the advent of modern technology for the Indians, including such conveniences as electricity and plastic goods, life will change quickly as the Maya enter the twenty-first century. Craftsmen such as this neighborhood shoe repairman will find themselves out of work. A hard-and-fast rule of the highland Indians is to buy as cheaply as one can, because *pisto* (money) is scarce. I have watched Indians bargain for over an hour just to save a few pennies.

On market day, high in the mountain village of
San Pedro Necta, a Mam Indian bargains for a
loaf of *panela* (brown sugar).

223

A

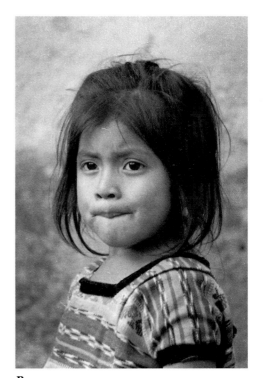

B

A–D. Four faces from the Guatemalan highlands: An old man from Todos Santos, high in the Cuchumatanes Mountains. A young girl from the village of Patzacía, near Antigua. A young boy, very nervous at his first sight of *extranjeros*. He lives on the mesa near Huehuetenango. A matron from San Juan Sacetepequez, embarrassed at the intrusion of the camera.

C

D

In troubled times, Maximon is often manifested in the guise of a powerful figure of authority such as the army general shown here.

This is a list of the colored candles and their significance as offerings to Maximon. From the top: Red for matters of love. Green for help in business. Blue for help in finding work. Pink for recovery from illness. Black for vengeance or placing curses on enemies. Light blue for money. (This one is very popular.) Purple for help in combating personal vices. Yellow for overall protection for adults. White paraffin for protection for children. Candles made from the fat of sheep (with a slight yellowish cast) for protection from spells cast by witches. Maximon is so deeply believed in by some, that I have seen men enter the temple with appropriate candles, burn them while shouting imprecations at each other (no law interferes here), and go into the nearest field and slash at one another with machetes.

Rare is the visitor who fails to be impressed with
the beauty of Lake Atitlan in the heart of the
Maya highlands.

For the Maya who still believe in old ways and day keepers, their world, according to prophecies, will end in the year 2012. In the meantime, they wait.

Sprawling across the great Maya site of Kaminaljuyu, the suburbs of Guatemala City now cover much of the site.

Surrounded by trees on a coffee finca known as La Chacra in Antigua, Guatemala, stand two monolithic stone heads. The how and why of these monuments remain a mystery. There are no apparent pyramids or other structures near them. This stone, assigned a Cotzumalhuapan style, was thought by archaeologist Eric Thompson to be an effigy of Huehueteotl, the old Mexican fire god.

The smaller of the two monuments at Finca La Chacra. No one seems to know or remember the occasion of the knocked-off nose.

232

Opposite above: These *muñecas* (dolls) from the hut of an Indian family at Chimaltenango, stare in wonder. Maya artists were very adept at portraying expressions.

Opposite below: The floor plan of Iximche, after being razed by the Spaniards during the conquest. This setting is one of the most beautiful in all of Guatemala.

Above: Defenders of Iximche fought off invaders from the top of the Fortress. The structure is solid, with no interior.

Above: The great ball court at Zaculeu.

Opposite: The likeness of the hated Spaniard Pedro Alvarado, or Tinatua, as the Indians called him, is the main figure in the Dance of the Conquistadors. Nearly every village in the highlands holds fiestas featuring Alvarado and his men in some way.

235

Maximon, depicted as an alcalde, or mayor, at his temple shrine in Iztapa, near the town of Antigua.

Maximon, or San Simone, is also known as Judas. Just to be on the safe side, modern Indians revile and sometimes hang the Judas figure at Easter time.

BIBLIOGRAPHY

Adams, Richard E. W. 1991. *Prehistoric Meso-america.* Rev. ed. Norman: University of Oklahoma Press.

———, ed. 1977. *Origins of Maya Civiliza-tion.* Albuquerque: University of New Mex-ico Press.

Andrews, George F. 1975. *Maya Cities: Place-making and Organization.* Norman: Univer-sity of Oklahoma Press.

Anton, Ferdinand 1970. *Art of the Maya.* New York: G. P. Putnam.

Ashmore, W., and R. J. Sharer 1978. "Excava-tions at Quiriguá, Guatemala: The Ascent of the Elite Maya Center." *Archaeology.* 31, no. 6.

Brennan, Louis A. 1974. *Beginner's Guide to Archaeology.* New York: Dell Publications.

Bullard, W. J., Jr., ed. 1975. Monographs and Papers on Maya Archaeology. Cambridge, Mass.: Peabody Museum Press.

Bunch, Roger, and Rolland Buch 1977. *The Highland Maya.* Visalia: Calif.: Josten's Pub-lications.

Burbank, Addison 1939. *Guatemala Profile.* New York: Van Rees Press.

Cerwin, Herbert 1963. *Bernal Diaz: Histo-rian of the Conquest.* Norman: University of Oklahoma Press.

Coe, Michael D. 1991. *The Maya: Ancient Peoples and Places.* Rev. ed. New York: Thames and Hudson.

———. 1992. *Breaking the Maya Code.* New York: Thames and Hudson.

Coe, William R. 1967. *Tikal: A Handbook of the Ancient Maya Ruins.* Philadelphia: University of Pennsylvania Museum.

———. 1975. "The Maya: Resurrecting the Grandeur of Tikal." *National Geographic* 148, no. 6.

Culbert, T. Patrick 1974. *Lost Civilization: The Story of the Classic Maya.* New York: Harper and Row.

Gallenkamp, Charles 1985. Maya: *The Riddle and Rediscovery of a Lost Civilization.* 3d ed. New York: Viking Penguin.

Graham, Ian 1967. *Archaeological Explorations in El Petén, Guatemala.* Cambridge, Mass.: Peabody Museum Press.

Graham, John A. 1966. *Ancient Mesoamerica: Selected Readings.* Palo Alto, Calif.: Peek Press.

Greene, Merle, Robert Rands, and John Graham 1972. *Maya Sculpture.* Berkeley: Lederer, Street, and Zeus.

Hammond, Norman 1988. *Ancient Maya Civilization.* 3d ed. Austin: University of Texas Press.

Hunter, Bruce 1974. *A Guide to Ancient Maya Ruins.* Norman: University of Oklahoma Press.

Kelley, David H. 1976. *Deciphering the Maya Script.* Austin: University of Texas Press.

Kelly, Joyce 1982. *The Complete Visitor's Guide to Mesoamerican Ruins.* Norman: University of Oklahoma Press.

Meyer, Karl E. 1973. *The Plundered Past.* Toronto: McClelland and Stewart.

Michel, Genevieve 1989. *The Rulers of Tikal.* Guatemala City: Publicaciones Vista.

Morley, Sylvanus G. 1935. *Guide Book to the Ruins of Quirigua.* Washington, D.C.: Carnegie Institution of Washington.

———. 1975. *An Introduction to the Study of the Maya Hieroglyphs.* New York: Dover.

Morley, Sylvanus G., and George W. Brainerd 1946. *The Ancient Maya.* 3d ed. Stanford, Calif.: Stanford University Press.

Parsons, Lee A. 1969. *Bilbao, Guatemala: An Archaeological Study of Pacific Coast Cotzumalhuapa Region.* Milwaukee Public Museum Publications in Anthropology, nos. 11 and 12.

Proskouriakoff, Tatiana 1963. *An Album of Maya Architecture.* Norman: University of Oklahoma Press.

Recinas, Adrién, and Delia Goetz 1953. *The Annals of the Cakchiqueles: Title of the Lords of Totonicapan.* Norman: University of Oklahoma Press.

Robicsek, Francis 1975. *A Study in Maya Art and History: The Mat Symbol.* New York: Museum of the American Indian.

Roys, Ralph L. 1975. *The Book of Chilam Balam of Chumayel.* Norman: University of Oklahoma Press.

Schele, L., and D. Friedel 1990. *A Forest of Kings.* New York: William Morrow and Co.

Soustelle, Jacques 1984. *The Olmecs.* New York: Doubleday.

Stuart, George E., and S. Gene Stuart 1977. *The Mysterious Maya.* Washington, D.C.: The National Geographic Society.

Stone, Doris 1972. *Pre-Columbian Man Finds Central America.* Cambridge, Mass.: Peabody Museum Press.

Tedlock, Dennis 1985. *Popol Vuh: A Translation.* New York: Simon and Schuster.

Thompson, J. Eric S. 1954. *The Rise and Fall of Maya Civilization.* Norman: University of Oklahoma Press.

———. 1963. *Maya Archaeologist.* Norman: University of Oklahoma Press.

———. 1970. *Maya History and Religion:* Norman: University of Oklahoma Press.

Time-Life, eds. 1993. *The Magnificent Maya.* Alexandria, VA.: Time-Life Books.

Tozzer, Alfred M., ed. 1975. *Landa's Relación de las Cosas de Tucatan: A Translation.* Cambridge, Mass.: Peabody Museum Press.

VanKirk, J., and Parney VanKirk, with Patricia de Solis 1992. *The World of Tikal.* 4th ed. St. Petersburg, Fla.: Great Outdoors Publishing Co.

Von Winning, Hasso 1968. *Pre-Columbian Art of Mexico and Central America.* New York: Abrams.

Wright, Ronald 1989. *Time Among the Maya.* New York: Weidenfeld and Nicholson.

INDEX

Unless otherwise noted, all locations are in Guatemala. References to legends are in italic type.

Abaj Takalik, 4–5, 9; Monument 1, *10, 34*
Adams, R. E. W., 56
Aguas Calientes, 67
Aguateca, 67, 68–69; emblem hieroglyph, *142;* Stela 1, *142;* Stela 2, *191;* Stela 3, *191;* Stela 68, *144*
Ah Cacau Caan Chac, *106, 107, 117*
Alvarado, Gonzales, 201
Alvarado, Pedro, 62, 63, 198, 199, 200, 201, 202, 203, *234*
Andrade, Fernando (foreign minister of Guatemala), 56
Antigua, 68, 79, 203, *230*
Antiquities, Maya, 56
Arroyo de Piedra, 67, 68, *142;* Stela 2, 68
Arroyo Itzan, 66
Atitlan, Lake, *215, 221, 227*
Atlatl, 70
Aviateca, 64
Aztec, 201, *207*

Ball court, *121, 234*
Ball player, *79, 86, 152*
Barba amarilla, 16, 153, 195
Basil Museum (Switzerland), *106*
Bejuco de Agua, 61, *181*
Belize, 53, 54, 55
Berendt, Carl Herman, 5, 6
Berlin (Germany), 6
Bilbao, 5, *20, 21, 22, 23;* Crab God, *23;* Los Gemalas, *23;* Monument 18, *22;* Monument 19, *20;* Monument 21, *21*

Brady, James, 52, *160*
Brady, Sandra, *160*
Britain, 57
British Honduras, 54. *See also* Belize
Bullard, James, 58

Cacao, 7, *16, 17, 21, 38;* god of, 6, *16*
Cahyup, *211, 212*
Cakchiquel, Maya, 199–200, *209*
Canchecan, 50, *156*
Cancuen, *69;* ball court, *145;* marker, *145;*
    Stela 1, *144*
Carnegie Institute, 60, 65, 197
Castillo, Dacio, *192*
Cauac Sky, 7, *31, 32, 44*
Chichen Itza, 62
Chichicastenango, *76, 260*
Chicleros, 49, 61, *167, 181*
Chimaltenango, *233*
Chinautla, 202
Chultun, *113*
Classic period, 52
Codex, codices, 51, 60, 63
Coe, William, 59, 60, *86*
Collared peccary, 50, *160*
Colorado, Prisciliano, 69
Copan, 7
Corbeled arch, *102, 178*
Cortés, Hernán, 199
Cotzumalhuapa area, 6, *330*
Cuchumatanes (mountains), 201
Curl Nose, *113, 114*
Dart, 70
De Las Casas, Fray Bartolomé, 199
Dolores, 53
Dos Lagunas, 55, 56
Dos Pilas, 67–68, *105, 139, 140, 142, 191;* hi-
    eroglyphic stairway, *187;* Stela 1 (detail), *139;*
    Stela 2, *140;* Stela 16, *139;* Stela 17, *139;*
    step, bound prisoner, *188;* stone head, *188*
Dwarfs, 77, *141*

Early Classic, 69, *114, 115*
Earthquake (of 1976), *206*
Ehecatl, *27*
El Baul, 5, *15;* god of cacao, *16;* jaguar monu-
    ment, *15;* Monument 2, *19;* Monument 3,

18; Monument 4, *17;* Monument 26, *15;*
    skull carving, *16;* Stela 1, *13;* Stela 27, *14*
El Bejucal, 61, *123, 180, 181*
El Caribe, 67
El Castillo, Finca, 5, *25, 26, 27*
El Cerritos, *28*
El Chal, 53; stela, *165, 166*
El Jobo, 3–4
El Naranjo, 54, 57, 64; Monument 25, *98;*
    Stela 10, *99;* Stela 20, *96;* Stela 25, *98;* Stela
    38, *98*
El Peru, 63–64, *126, 128;* long-nosed god, *127*
El Peten, 6, 49, 50, 53, 56, 57, 62, 63, 64, 65,
    66, 67, 69, 70, *96, 102, 103, 156, 158, 160,
    165, 171*
El Salvador, 6
El Zotz, 61–62, 69, *124;* El Templo del Dia-
    blo, 61
Esquintla, 5
Esso Company, 68

Fer-de-lance. *See Barba amarilla*
Fernandez de Oviedo, Gonzales, *38*
Finca San Francisco, stone carving, *24, 41*
Flores, 53, 62, *105. See also* Tayasal
France, 57
Fulgorid, peanut headed, *102*
FYDEP (Fomentación y Desarrollo El
    Petén), *96, 98*

Graham, Ian, 54, 67, *136*
Graham, John, 4, 5, *153*

Halach uinic, 128
Harvard University, *147*
Hero Twins, *82, 86*
Highlands, 197
Honduras, 6–7, 62
Hotun, *44, 64*
Huehueteotl, *230. See also* El Baul
Hunahpu (Hero Twin), *82, 86*

Iguana, 3, *11*
Itsimte, 66; Stela 4, *134*
Itza, 62, 63, *203*
Itzam Na, *11*
Itzan, 66–67, *134*

Iximche, 199–201, *233*

Ixkan Río, 55

Ixkun, 53; Stela 1, 53, *164*

Ixlu, 59; Altar 1, *105;* Stela 2, *105, 106*

Ixtutz, 52–53; Stela 1, *164*

Jade: mask, *42;* figure, *43*

Jaguar, *79, 80, 156;* altar, *204;* glyph, *80;* hieroglyphic panel, *80;* jaguar monument, *15;* Monument 26, *15;* myth, *160;* patron of number 7, *156*

Jaguar Paw Skull II (ruler of Tikal), *116*

Kaibal (king of Zaculeu), 201, 202

Kaminaljuyu, 197–98; jaguar altar, *204;* site mound, *229;* Stela 11, 206; toad altar, 205

Katun (twenty-year period), 57, 67, *111, 116*

Kekchi Maya, 50

Kinich Ahau (Maya sun god), *48, 100. See also* Quirigua

K'umarcaaj, 198–99, 201, *207. See also* Utatlan

La Amelia, 67; Stela 2, *136*

La Chacra, Finca, *230, 231*

La Democracia, 6, *28, 29*

La Florida, 64, *184;* Stela 9, 184

Lago Izabal, 6

Laguna Patixbatun, 68

Laguna San Diego, 65

Lahuntun, 67

La Libertad, 65, 66

La Reforma, 69

Las Illusiones, 5

Late Classic, 4, 5, 54, 55, 65, 67, 68, 77, *111, 139*

Late Formative, 5

La Victoria, 3–4

Long-nosed god, *115, 120, 127*

Lopez, Anatolio, 55

Los Duendes, 68, *140, 141*

Lowland Maya, *134*

Lowlands, 49

Macanche, 57, *171*

Machaquila, 69, 70, *191, 192;* Stela 3, *146;* Stela 4, *146;* Stela 7, *147;* Stela 9, *147*

Maize, 4

Maler, Teobert, 53, 57, 58, 62, 64, 66, 99, *113, 115*

Mam (Maya god), 4, 201, 203

Mam Maya, 4, *216, 223*

Mantis, banjo head leaf, *189*

Margay, *126*

Maudsley, Alfred P., 69

Maximon (Maya god), 203, *226, 236*

Maya gods, Itzam Na (creation god), *11;* Kinich Ahau (sun god), *48, 100;* long-nosed god, *115, 120, 127;* Mam, 4, 21, 203; Maximon, 203, *226, 236;* Tzimin Chac, 63; Yum Kaax (corn god), *151, 209*

Maya Mountains, 50, *158*

Mecapal, *75, 76*

Melchor de Mencos, 54, *98*

Mesoamerica, 5, 6

Mexican gods: Ehecatl (wind god), *27;* Huehueteotl (fire god), *230;* Nanahuatl (The Syphilitic One), 27; Tlaloc (rain god), *41, 103, 114;* Xipe Totec (god of flaying, of spring), *195*

Mexico, 5, 54, 63, *117*

Miles, S. W., *206*

Mixco Viejo, 202–203, *212, 214*

Monte Alto, 6, *28, 29*

Monument Plaza, 6

Mopan River, 52

Morley, Sylvanus, 67, *164, 195*

Motagua River, 7

Motagua valley, 7

Mot-mot, *46. See also* Myth

Motul de San José, 62, *183*

Museo Nacional (National Museum, Guatemala), *31*

Myths: dwarfs, *141;* fulgorid, peanut head, *102;* jaguar, *160;* mot-mot, *46;* scorpion, *133*

Naj Tunich, 50–52, *74, 88, 90, 94, 160;* Bearer of Fire Room, *75, 76, 77;* Chamber of Crystal Columns, *79;* dwarfs, *77;* Grand Concourse, *75, 77;* Hall of Balam, *79, 80;* Hall of Musicians, *77;* Hero Twins, *82, 86;* Jaguar glyph, *80;* Jaguar panel, *80;* Main Entrance Hall, *158, 160;* moon goddess, *84;* Passage of Rites, *84, 85, 87, 89;* sun god, *93;* tombs, *73*

Nal-Tel (corn), 4
Nakum, 57; Temple A, *102*
Nanahuatl (Mexican god), 27
Neutron activation analysis, 56

Ocos, 3–4
Ocultun, 64; Stela 9, *184*
Olmec, 5. *See* Jade
Oviedo y Valdez, Gonzalo Fernandez, *38*

Pacific Coast, 3, *33*
Pacific Ocean, 3
Palo Gordo, 5, *11, 35, 37*
Pantaleón, 5, *28;* Monument 1, *25, 26*
Parsons, Lee, 5, *20*
Patixbatun, 67, 68, *142, 188*
Peabody Museum (Harvard), 56, 57, 70, 71,
    154, 194
Peten Itza, Lake, 57, 62, 63, 203
Piedra Santa, 5, *12, 35, 37;* altar, *12*
Piedras Negras, 64–65, 70, *128, 130;* Stela 12,
    130; throne, *128;* Wall Panel 3, *128*
Pipil, 5
Poco Mam, 202
Polol, 65–66, *186;* Stela 2, *133*
Pop, Barnabé, 51
Pop, Emilio, 50, 51, *160*
Poptun, 52, 53, 70, *158*
Popul Vuh, 82, 86
Posole, 66
Postclassic, 77
Post-Olmec, 5, *10*
Potzun, *218*
Preclassic, 4, 67
Pre-Columbian, 67, *108*
Prensa Libre, 52
Pre-Olmec, 6, *29*
Proskouriakoff, Tatiana, 64
Puerto Barrios, 6, *139*

Quiche Maya, 4, *39,* 199–200
Quintal, *150*
Quirigua, 6–7, *31, 32, 44, 46, 48, 64;* Altar L,
    31; Cauac Sky, *31, 32;* Kinich Ahau, *48;*
    Motagua valley, 7; Stela I, *31;* Stela D, *46;*
    Stela E, *44;* Stela J, *32;* Stela K, *32;* zoo-
    morph P, *44*

Rabinal valley, *211, 212*
Retalhuleu, 4
Río Azul, 54–56, *99, 168;* burial niche, *100;*
    mat symbol, *100;* Kinich Ahau, *100;*
    Ruler X, *99, 100, 168*
Río Homul, 57, *102*
Río Lacantun, *150*
Río Pasión, 66, 67, 69, *150*
Río Salinas, *150*
Río San Pedro, 64
Río Usumacinta, *150*
Robertson, Merle Green, *134, 151*
Rocky Mountains, 4

Sacluk, 66
Sacul, 52, *95, 161*
San Andres Ixtapa (temple of Maximon), 203,
    236
San Diego, 65, *130, 133, 185*
San José de Motul, *183*
San Pedro Necta, *223*
Santa Cruz del Quiche, 199
Santa Elena, *96*
Santa Lucía Cotzumalhuapa, 5–6, *37*
Sayaxche, 67, 69, 70, *134, 136, 150*
Schultz, George (U.S. secretary of state),
    56
Scorpion, *133*
Sculptures, boulder, 6, *29, 34*
Seibal, 67, 70–71, *150, 151, 153, 154, 156,
    194, 196;* emblem glyph, *196;* jaguar table,
    154; late stela, *154;* Stela 1, *153;* Stela 3,
    151; Stela 7, *152;* Stela 8, *149;* Stela 9, *147;*
    Stela 10, *149;* Stela 11, *149;* Stela 13, *153;*
    Stela 14, *154;* Stela 19, *151–52;* Stela 21,
    195; stela segment (detail), *156;* temple,
    194; viewing stand, *154*
Shateros, 61
Shook, Edwin M., *29,* 59, 64, *118, 177*
Sierra de las Minas (mountains), 6
Sierra de Santa Cruz (mountains), 6
Sierra Madres (mountains), 4
Solola, *221*
South America, 4
South coast, 4
Spanish conquest, 62
Stormy Sky (ruler of Tikal), *114, 115*